THE BOX

Victim: Loss of Power

Gabriel Singleton

I Rise Publishing

PUBLISHING

Printed in the United States of America.

For more information, or to book an event, contact:
WeRise@IRisePublishing.com
https://www.irisepublishing.com/

Cover design by Ujala Shahid

ISBN - Paperback: 979-8-9900501-3-6

Second Edition: June 2024

Dedication

I would like to dedicate this book to my family. I would not have the life I have without you. My story would not be my story without you, both the good with the bad. Thank God that the good days now outweigh the bad. Thank you for forgiving me. Thank you for seeing me for who I am and not what I have done. And thank you to those who had the strength, courage, and understanding to not only change; but to come back and reconcile. I love you all so much! God bless you…

CONTENTS

NOTE: AN "*" INDICATES A POEM

* D e c l a r a t i o n o f L o v e

If I ever have you, though chances might be slim
I want your life to be bright, not dark, not dim
I want you to know that if I have a child
I'll protect you, mind-body-spirit, I want your innocence to
be wild
I want you to be free, curious, and active everyday
And never fear to tell me what it is you need to say
Your imaginations flowing from above and not below
Let my patience run for miles and my anger come slow
That my overprotectiveness not bring you too much
frustration
But know that I love you by this demonstration
May you never lack the comfort of my kisses and hugs
And my arms forever be a place of safety and love
Let the words of my mouth be encouraging and constructive
And the actions you see be positive and productive
I wear my heart on my sleeve for all who look to see
I want you to be my future and not how I used to be

Written by,
Gabriel Singleton

10/4/17

* The Constant Contemplation

My past has a death grip on my mind.
How many times do I sit and wish I could rewind time?
But time stands still for no man.
Oh man, sitting here hoping destiny is definitely in His hands.
Cause these hands can't move alone.
Only He leaves breath in this body so I can call earth my home.
My dome would split with the weight of it.
But, thank God, He holds the glue to keep this hard-headed skull from getting a crack in it.
Whacking it up against the wall is what I wish I could do cause when I blacken it, my life won't be blue.
But roses will always be red.
And hell is hotter than P.I. in the summer so, I don't wish I was dead.
The bread of life is what sustains me.
Suicidal thoughts are squashed by the recompense of taking my life for me.
What it's like for me? You'll never know.
Cause walking in my shoes eventually you'd be taking a different road.
We're not the same, we would never be.
Cause God created us different, as far as the West is from the East.

So, let me breathe for a minute.
That's all we have in this world cause once we turn around
our lives will be ending.
I can't change what I've done in the past.
But as I breathe I can change, even when I get down to my
last.
They say make your haters your motivators.
To everyone that hates me, I'm sorry that you were part of
my education.
Cause the lessons that I've learned are for life.
I've been abused since my birth, it's not easy to let it burn.
I took a turn for the worse,
When I decided, as a little girl, that I would indulge in this
family curse.
If you can't beat'em then join'em, right?
Wrong! Cause you might get caught up and be the only one
that still can't get right.
Aint no use in pointing fingers.
Cause there's three pointing right back at you and they
sound off as loud as a Derringer.
I had to get it from somewhere.
But now I'm sitting here thinking that I was born to be
tempted to go there.
So, now I wish the cord had choked me.
So, I wouldn't have to deal with myself and all the things
that I thought provoked me.
But I broke free from the chains
That surround me and bound me to a life of open disdain
Of the shameful things that I was doing.
Pursuing death with every step, but every day now it's life

that I'm choosing.

CHAPTER 1

LOCKDOWN

This poem was written from my cell in solitary lockdown. At this point I am twenty-four years old and in prison for child molestation. Did I do it? Yes. I have no qualms about admitting to it. I molested my nephew and this is how it all began…

When Simeon was born, I was 12 years old. My sister Samantha was 18 at the time. I don't think she was well equipped, mentally, to handle a baby. At this point we lived in Georgia, but she moved back and forth between Georgia and Louisiana about every six months or so.

When she lived here she left Simeon with my mother most of the time. My mother who still had 5 kids to raise and worked a full-time job. So, most of the responsibility of taking care of him when he was at our apartment was left to me.

I started wondering things about babies when I would change his diaper or take him a bath. I wondered whether baby boys could get aroused at such a young age with stimulation. What triggered that thought for me was that his penis would always stand up when he was getting ready to urinate. That was always my cue to hurry up and put a diaper on him.

He was about 9 or 10 months old when I decided to test that theory out. Needless to say, it worked and I got aroused by it also. That day was the start of the path I chose to walk down. I was 13 when I started molesting my nephew.

When he was a baby I'd touch him almost every day. It was either during bath time, when I would change his diaper or bedtime because he'd usually sleep with me. Between the ages of one and two he started to touch himself without any influence from me.

He'd do it when someone changed his diaper, during his bath time, or sometimes when he would be trying to go to sleep. At first my other siblings around my age thought it was funny. His mother even took a picture of him sleeping with his penis hanging out of his diaper.

It was all humorous until one of my older sisters, Rachel, brought it up that he does that too often for it to be normal. She'd say someone must have been touching him in that way for him to keep doing that. Then she started asking him around two years old who was touching his penis like that. He pointed directly at me and said his version of my name, "Babbell."

That's when I began to get scared. I laughed it off and lied and said I wasn't doing anything out of the ordinary. I made the point that I was the one who bathed him everyday and changed his diapers. Of course, he would point me out because I do have to touch him there on a daily basis.

His mother dismissed it as nothing and that I was right and she continued to leave him with me. From then on out though, Rachel always looked at me suspiciously. I took steps to cover my tracks. I stopped touching him as often and I coached him on what to say when he was questioned about someone touching his penis.

Eventually, he stopped saying it was me and started to keep what I did to him to himself. He learned from me that it was a secret between the both of us and he couldn't tell or else we would get into trouble and I'd go away for a long time. I'd ask him if he wanted me to go away and he'd always say no and I'd tell him that he had to keep our secret if he didn't want me to go away and be punished.

Things progressed from me just touching him to hunching him naked in that area. Things never progressed beyond the touching and hunching. It would always start with the touching followed by the hunching. He would never seek me out to do these things, and he would never tell me no. I would ask him periodically and he'd say he liked it.

As I got older I'd touch him less and less. It went from almost every day to once a week. Then down to once or twice a month. By the time he was ten it had gotten down to every four or five months. My interests had changed. I had moved on to wanting different things, but I would always go back to molesting him.

Added to that was the hatred. I would prefer my other nieces and nephews over him. I'd spend more time with them than I did him. Whenever he did something wrong I would whip him twice as hard as I would the others, if I even whipped them at all. There was definitely a marked difference in the way I treated him. Even family members noticed and I would always attribute it to the fact that he was always there at the house so he got on my nerves more often.

When he and his mother lived with us I would constantly get into arguments with her. I wanted her to move out. When she finally did he was about 5 or 6. But even still he got off the bus there every day and practically spent the summers and holidays with us. So, I abused him still.

When he was ten years old they had sex education in his class at school. They talked to the students about good touch and bad touch. They expressed to them that if they were experiencing bad touch from someone that they needed to tell someone about it.

He went home that day and told his mother that I had been touching him. By that evening, I was confronted by my mother with what he had confessed. I didn't say a word to her either way. I just went into my room.

The next day I went outside to wash the car and mom decided to come out and help me. She got up the nerve to ask me outright if I had done what Simeon had said. I stopped, took a deep breath, and told her yes. She stood there for a minute looking at me and then turned, went into the house to get her purse, and she left.

Two weeks later I went to speak to an investigator about the charges brought up against me. I told him the truth about everything. I was arrested that day. It was a Friday in February 2004 and I was released out on bond to my mother that Monday morning.

A year later, in May of 2005, I was sentenced to fifteen years, serving three in prison. I began my incarceration a week after the sentencing.

My life is a complicated one in some ways, but very simple in others. I'd like to share my story with you, not only for myself, but for others. Others that are like me and those that are not. I understand that this is a very controversial, emotional, and difficult subject. I also think that now is a great time for people's eyes to be opened to the whole truth and not just one part of the story. I can only hope that those who start this journey with me will stick it out to the end.

CHAPTER 2

MY FIRST MEMORY

"Go tell your daddy the food ready," Momma said. At the time, she had lived her whole life in Louisiana so, you can imagine the accent that came with that statement. The shocker was that she was talking to me. I was about three years old. Momma had never told me to do something so responsible before.

To understand the gravity of this situation you'd have to understand the inner workings of my family. Daddy was law. Anything and everything he said and did was the rule. There was no negotiation around it. What was worse was that if you messed something up, something as simple as a message, it could rouse his anger. Then, all hell would break loose on your behind. I had to get this right.

If daddy was ever at home, you would usually find him in one of two places in our house, their bedroom or the living room. In this case, it was the bedroom. To get there, I had to walk from the kitchen down to the end of that hallway. Their room was at the end to the left, just before it was another hallway to the right. There were two rooms down there, my grandmothers' room and the room my four brothers occupied.

This hallway had no windows, the further you went, the darker it got. I started my trek down repeating the message like a mantra, hoping that I wouldn't forget it. It was so simple, but at that age it was very difficult for me to keep things together in my mind for long. Before I could make it pass the hallway to the right I was grabbed and a hand was put over my mouth to keep me quiet.

I was dragged immediately to the end of the hallway outside of my brothers' room. Someone whispered, "Go down to the end of the hallway and look out while I have my turn, then we'll switch." The voice was from my older brother, Daniel. As my eyes adjusted to the dark, I realized that he was talking to my brother, Derrick. Daniel was three years older than me and Derrick, a year younger than him.

Everything happened very quickly after that. Daniel pushed me down to the floor and proceeded to get on top of me, still holding my mouth. At this point I was trying desperately to tell him I had something important to do. He shushed me and began to hunch me. Even with all of our clothes on I could feel his penis prodding against the front of my private area.

I was not shocked at this, which leads me to believe it had happened before. I was more concerned with what would happen if my message didn't reach our father in an appropriate amount of time. I was scared to death of what would happen so I began to fight him. I was pushing and slapping and hitting, but to no avail. He didn't budge. He just kept his hand over my mouth and continued to grind.

After a while, Derrick returned asking when it was going to be his turn. Daniel, still hunching, grunted out that he wasn't finished yet and he should go back to keeping a lookout, he'd come to get him when he was done. Derrick wasn't satisfied with this answer, so they began to argue in heated whispers.

"What's going on down here?" Everyone froze in terror, eyes wide with fear as the light in the hallway came on. It was my father. Immediately, like string puppets, my brothers were up and standing ramrod straight facing him. I got up a little slower. I was fearful of him, but I felt that I was in less trouble than they were. As soon as I was on my feet I pointed a finger at them both and opened my mouth.

That was as far as I had gotten. In the few seconds it took for me to stand, Daddy had already taken off his belt. By the time I had gotten my mouth open and turned my eyes from my brothers to him, he was in mid-swing. But the belt wasn't aimed at my brothers. I was off to the side, but still a little further in front of them.

I didn't have enough time to brace myself for the onslaught. No time to run, no time to tense up and squeeze my eyes shut. What I remember most was the look on Daddy's face. It was a mixture of anger, hatred, and disgust. His eyes exuded it. His mouth was a testament to it, bottom lip tucked in with his teeth biting into it with an intensity that seemed like it would draw blood.

There was grunting and words and screaming with each swing. When you put all the words together they basically meant that he was tired of me messing with his boys. That was always the message from then on out. The screams though, they weren't all coming from me. We were all stuck in one little group in the corner at the end of that hallway. Though his anger was mainly concentrated on me, my brothers did catch some of the lashes from his belt swing.

It felt like it would never end. When each swing made contact, it set off a wave of pain that seemed like it registered through my entire body. With each passing minute, my strength waned. I was unprepared for this. I'd try my best not to do this but it always happened when I was caught off guard with a whipping. As it goes on I begin to lose control of my bodily functions. This was one of those times.

One stroke caused a little stream of warm liquid to start to expand in my underwear. With the next one it trickled down my legs as all of my muscles began to shake uncontrollably. Fear gripped me as, with the third, a puddle gathered at my feet. At that point, my father noticed and stopped to stare in disgust at the mess I'd made.

One of two things always happened in moments like these. He'd either be completely revolted and walk away or what I'd done would enrage him further and the whipping would continue with even more vehemence. I was praying for the former. God answered my prayer that day, and with a last look of loathing, he walked away shaking his head.

I don't remember anything beyond him walking away.

But what still resonates within me is my disappointment, my anger, the unfairness about the entire situation, and how powerless I was to do anything about it. And most of all, I will never forget the look on my father's face.

CHAPTER 3

WHIPPINGS

I was raised in an abusive family; mentally, physically, sexually, financially, and emotionally. There's not a lot about my past that I can look back on and smile or laugh about. I fight depression every day, but I can say that most days the things I get sad about now are miniscule compared to the past. But even so, sometimes the sadness gets the best of me. When you've lived a life like I have, a lot of the time, you are an observer of happiness instead of a participant. It's hard for me to feel happy when there's a weight on living each day. Weights that I have put on myself, mostly, because it's truly up to me to let it go.

I had my first memory at the age of three. I think that day stuck with me because it was so unpleasant. After that I don't really remember most of the times that I got whippings. I know that they happened, but only a few stuck with me.

I remember once when I was about six and I was outside playing with my brothers, Daniel and Derrick. You see, my mother had ten children for my father, four boys and six girls. I was number eight in the order and surrounded by boys on either side. Daniel and Derrick are numbers six and seven, Matthew is the last boy coming in at number nine.

I played with my brothers a lot because we were closer in age. I would always want to go out and play with my brothers, even if sometimes it ended up with us hunching. All except for Charlie who was the second child born to my mother, he was a lot older.

By this age, I was no longer indifferent to it, I liked it. Especially when they invited their friend Tommy over to play. He was the little white boy who lived behind us. I liked Tommy because he liked to hunch also and because he wasn't my brother. He came over that day and we decided to play underneath a truck camper that my father had laid on the ground. At first it was normal stuff like playing marbles or wrestling, but eventually it turned to hunching.

When we got caught my father was furious. So much so that he lifted that camper up with one hand and flipped it over. He also whipped Tommy right along with us. He whipped him all the way home. After that Tommy never came out to play with us again. I was sad about that because I really liked Tommy more than I did my brothers.

Every whipping wasn't about getting caught doing something sexual though. Most of the other ones I got were just like any other, they didn't make any sense to me. For instance, our next-door neighbor bred dogs. She didn't like it when we fed them bones and table food through her fence. So, she had told my father and he told us never to do so. He also told us not to touch her dogs.

Well, one day when we had gotten off the bus from

school we saw that her puppies had dug a hole in the fence and gotten out. Daniel and Derrick decided that they were going to go put the puppies back in the fence. I quickly ran into the house, threw my book bag on the living room floor, and ran out to help.

As we were putting the puppies back into the fence we heard, "What y'all doin' over there!" All three of us froze, that voice was our father's, he was not supposed to be home yet. My brother Daniel told me to go explain to him what we were doing. I was afraid, I was always afraid to say anything to him. But Daniel was under the impression that there's no way we could be in trouble for helping. So, I walked over to him, heart pounding in my chest and all ready with an explanation.

"Don't come lying on my boys, go to your room!" he said. I was shocked. He actually thought I was coming over to lie on my brothers, how absurd! What was also confusing was that he told me to go to my room. My father had never used solitary confinement as a punishment. I was baffled. One thing I knew for sure, though, I'd better do what he said and be quick about it.

There was only one problem with that, I had left my book bag on the living room floor. In his house, if you ever placed something where it did not belong, that was cause for an automatic whipping. So, I ran into the living room to get my book bag and as I turned around to make my way up the stairs, I stopped dead in my tracks. He had followed me inside and was now taking off his belt.

"Didn't I tell you to go upstairs?" There was no way around this one. I hated that belt. It was brown and heavy and leather, and it hurt just as bad as the extension cord. Before I could even get the first word out for an explanation that belt was already up in the air, poised and ready for its downward swing. I was older now and my reaction time was quicker.

I balled my hands into fists, hunched my shoulders up, put that slight bend in my knees, and squeezed my eyes shut. I was ready. And I was also angry. It didn't make any sense to get a whipping for something so stupid. That day I think my anger took away my ability to feel and I was glad for it. I did not feel a thing, except for the anger.

Afterwards he sent me upstairs anyway. I remember being so angry over the whole ordeal. I went up to my room that I shared with two other sisters. I sat down on the bed and I looked at my legs. That's when I began to feel again. I had welts all over my legs and my arms. They had swelled up so much so that little beads of blood were starting to form at the edges on either side.

That's when I felt the stinging, like bees had lined up in rows on my arms and legs and decided to sting in unison. At that moment, I can say that I really started to hate my Dad. He never tried to understand anything. All he did was whip, whip, whip. Even if he found out that he was wrong later, he would never go back and apologize. Like, no matter what he did, it was always the right thing to do because he answered to no one. I sat in the room and cried for hours that day.

Then there was the one that I will never forget. I was about eight. Derrick approached me very earnestly and said, "I'm going to stop messing with you." He didn't have to say specifically what that meant, I knew. I asked him why and he told me that it was because it wasn't right. He told me that we should not be doing these things. He also said that he thought I should stop letting Daniel do it to me as well. He said that if he wouldn't stop after I asked, that I should tell on him. I told him okay, but I was sad that Derrick didn't want to do these things anymore because I liked it with him more than I did Daniel.

The next time Daniel approached me wanting to hunch I told him that I didn't want to do it anymore. He asked why and I told him about what Derrick had said. He listened and then told me okay, but that we were just going to do it this once and then he would quit. And for a while that's how it would always happen with him, just this one time and then we'll quit.

Finally, I got up the nerve to tell my mother. I told her that Daniel was messing with me. She asked me how and I told her in a nasty way. I told her that he was putting his "thing" on my privates and I wanted him to stop. She said okay, but she didn't immediately call him or say anything to him. I was a little confused about that one. But I figured she'd handle it in her own time. Mom always had a lot to do. She was always busy, so I left it alone.

Later that day my father approached me and asked,

"What's this I hear about you saying that Daniel keeps touching you? Didn't I tell you to stop messing with my boys?" Fear, horror, shock, and most of all, betrayal all went through my mind at once. My mother had told my father. That was her way of handling the situation. I should've known. How could I be so stupid to trust her? All day I'd had a sick feeling in my stomach as if something wasn't right about her reaction.

As always, I was not given a chance to answer. In the first place, how could you answer questions that clearly said you were the culprit and a liar? I only remember that I did get a whipping, but that's it. I didn't feel a thing. I don't remember the aftermath of the welts or anything else. It went on like that for the rest of my years living with my father. I'd remember what led up to the whippings, the hatred and disgust in his eyes, the biting of his bottom lip. I just never remembered what happened afterward.

I had waited a while after that and tried once more to tell my mother. I even asked her not to tell my dad and asked if she could talk to Daniel herself. She had said okay, but then she told my father anyway. It ended like it always did. From that point on I really felt like I couldn't beat him, so I joined him.

CHAPTER 4

CONFINEMENT

After the episode with Tommy, my father was so furious that he told my mother and all my sisters that I was never to be let outside again unless I was with one of my sisters or my mother. I was forbidden to play with my brothers outside. He was determined that I was to stop messing with his boys. My dad was under the impression that I was the perpetrator in these situations no matter that they were older than I was. To my father, I was the child version of a whore.

As far back as I can remember, my mother was never the type to go against anything my father said. He would set down the rules, whatever they were, and she would follow them. She never seemed to question anything he did, which made everything he did seem like it must be okay. It made me feel as if all households were the same.

Days were so long then, unbelievably long. I lived for school. In the summer times, I felt like I would die of boredom. My days were filled with watching my mother cook and clean, helping her fold clothes, or feeling like I was going to go crazy because the only thing on television on the weekdays were the soap operas my mother loved to watch.

The only good times were when it rained, Saturday mornings, and after dinner. Those were the only times my other siblings were around to play with and Saturday mornings were filled with cartoons, so my brothers stayed inside until noon.

I was very active as a child. I climbed trees, wrestled, played baseball, basketball, and ran just about everywhere. My Dad was a bricklayer and we used to make things with his scaffolding because we were so bored. He didn't believe in buying toys, he was too cheap for that. My brothers and I used to climb on top of the roof just to jump off it for fun. I was a tomboy through and through. So, you can imagine what being inside felt like to me, prison. There was no running or jumping or climbing, there was only sitting and being quiet.

Because I didn't go outside often, this led to obnoxious behavior. My sister Reagan, who is four years older than me, was the closest girl and was tasked to take me outside when she would go out. But Reagan loved to read books so most of the time she was up in our room reading. When she wasn't reading, I was being a brat to her as much as I could, the duty of a normal younger sibling. Because of this, Reagan would wait until I had taken a bath to go out and spend time with her friends.

The rule was, if you had already taken a bath for the day, you could no longer go outside. A six or seven-year old really doesn't grasp the fact that if you were nicer to your sister you could go out more often. I had so much energy on the inside of me that it was literally impossible for me not to get on her nerves at some point. It was almost as if I couldn't help it.

Needless to say, for the next three years or so I didn't go out much. It didn't change the fact that sexual things still happened, they just always happened in the house from there on out. I started to gain weight because I wasn't active enough throughout the day. I was sad and bored most of the time. There wasn't much to do besides chores. I became a master at folding clothes and by age ten I was considered a little chubby.

The only good memory from my confinement was when I was about seven, my dad went away to work in another state for almost the entire summer. I worked on my mother every single day to let me go outside. I absolutely begged on my knees day in and day out. It took her about three days of that to give in. I broke loose like a wild animal. Every day, as soon as I brushed my teeth, got dressed, and ate breakfast I was out the door. Aside from lunch, I would stay outside all day until the sun went down.

I ran, I wrestled with my brothers, we played marbles with their friends. I climbed trees, swung off branches. We played in the rain. We'd eat watermelon outside and chase each other down to spit seeds at one another. We talked my mother into buying us a kiddy pool. It had a six-foot diameter and it could hold water a foot deep. We filled it up in the front yard, placed it close to the roof and proceeded to jump off the roof into that pool until we broke it about two or three days later.

We begged her to buy us another one, a deeper one. She adamantly told us no, but after about two weeks we wore her down. She bought us one that had a diameter of nine feet and it was two feet deep, it came with the warning that if we broke it she wouldn't buy another. We decided that jumping off the roof wasn't a good idea and this one lasted about two weeks.

Even my mother was a different person when my father was gone. She let us do a lot of things we couldn't do when he was around and every time he called she told him everything was fine. I was shocked. She never told him that she let me go outside with the boys or any of the other stuff she let us do that he wouldn't approve of. She even laughed with us sometimes. Our friends were invited over to play in our yard, Dad never let us do that. She drew the line at them coming into the house though.

Then one day she sat us all down and told us that he was coming back the next day. She didn't have to explain what that meant. Everything was going to have to go back to normal. The next day was all doom and gloom. Everyone was walking around the house with sad faces. My mother was quietly moving through the house like even she was sad about his return.

I held a small hope that he wouldn't make it back. That he would get into a car accident, or something, and die. I'd always wished that my father would just die some horrible death. But as always, our ears picked up the rumble of his truck as he rounded the corner down the street.

Everyone scrambled for a spot on the sofa, like usual. We waited for him to come inside and speak. We all spoke back in unison and things went back to normal again. My mother never told my father that she let me out of the house. I was so relieved and grateful for that.

CHAPTER 5

LIVING IN FEAR

Matthew was almost a year younger than me, but not quite. My mother had him prematurely, so we stayed the same age for a week out of the year before I'd make my birthday. One day when I was very young, I'd say five or six, my mother took Matthew to the doctor. She came back very upset, something was wrong. Matthew had an STD.

It was explained to me through my older siblings that that wasn't a good thing. Matthew was too young to have an STD because only grown-ups got stuff like that from having sex with someone who had it. We were all told about it and we were, all nine of us, going to be tested for the same thing. They had to find out how he had gotten this.

By this time, I was very afraid. I just had a feeling that this was all going to fall on me. That I was going to be the one that had contracted the same disease. I knew as soon as Dad found out that, this time, he might actually kill me. This was serious, doctors had gotten involved. The school had gotten involved.

I was called to the office and spoken to by a very nice lady and the principal during this time. I vaguely remember my dad having a talk with me about the people coming to the school. I don't remember the conversation exactly. I just remember being threatened with a whipping if I said something wrong.

That lady was very nice, but she lied about one thing. She told me that it was okay to say anything I liked and that I wouldn't get in trouble for it. From then on, I knew not to trust her because she didn't know my daddy. I didn't care what she said, he'd get me, he always did.

· · ·

When I knew I was going to get a whipping, sometimes I'd run away from him, I'd get a good distance between us because I knew he wouldn't chase me. I'd run like hell. But my father had a secret weapon, Daniel and Derrick. They were like his two guard dogs. All he'd have to say was, "Go get her!" They'd come running, gaining on me like predators.

I don't think they enjoyed chasing me, but for fear of getting a beating themselves, they would make haste. No matter how hard I tried I could never get away. With feet pumping as hard as my heart, I would run in despair, knowing they would catch me, prolonging the inevitable.

If it was outside, they would drag me back kicking and screaming. If I ran up the stairs they'd catch me before I'd reach the top. They would pry my fingers away from whatever rung I was holding on to and drag me back down the stairs, my crying interrupted by the bump of each step. All the while he'd be waiting, sometimes with a smirk as if to say, "I'll show you what running will get you." At other times, he would be waiting with what looked like pure hatred in his eyes.

. . .

She just didn't know what she was up against, this nice lady. She asked a lot of questions, but I wasn't stupid. I know what she really wanted to know. They'd come out like harmless questions, "Do you play doctor at home with your brothers and sisters?" I'd told her yes, which was the truth. But when she would ask what we did when we played doctor, I lied.

I told her we'd use some of my daddy's tools as doctor tools. I described to her how we would use them, like any normal child with a healthy, innocent imagination. She seemed very pleased with all my answers. I don't think she even realized that I was smarter than what I let on. All my father's children were smart as a whip, just like him, most of us just weren't crazy like he was.

When I got home that day there was no whipping waiting for me. I must have passed the test. But there was the other one left, that one I knew I would fail. We had an appointment scheduled to go see the doctor.

When we got there, I want to say they took us into the room two at a time and matched us up by age. I got paired with my little sister Karen, she was one or two at the time. All I can remember is being nervous, wondering what they were going to do to us, what would my fate be after the results of this day?

I remember the doctor telling my mother how fast my heart was beating when he put his hand over my chest. He assumed that I was afraid of the procedure and tried to calm me down by talking to me and telling me what he was going to do. All he did was take a q-tip and swabbed it around down there.

When it came to my baby sister though, she was very ticklish in that area and she just laughed and laughed. She kept squeezing her legs closed when she'd feel the q-tip and she just kept laughing. The doctor had to keep trying because she wouldn't let him get a good swab. I want to say she thought it was a game. She laughed so loudly that you could hear her outside the room, people made comments about it later.

I stayed in a constant state of fear during that entire time. It lasted a few days. When the results came back I was shocked. None of us had what Matthew had. It remained a mystery from then on out. Everyone was wondering how he could contract something like that and no one else had gotten it. It's a good thing that whatever it was, it was curable. He took medicine for it and I never heard anything else about it. Imagine my relief, to find out that it wasn't me after all.

. . .

Another time my mom's sister talked her into coming to see some prophetess. I think my mom's mother had thirteen children; I'm not sure because my mom isn't even sure about that one. Mom had a lot of sisters. This was the youngest of them all and I always thought she was quite a bit different than the others. She could read for one, unlike my mother and father.

She spoke differently and always seemed to have an uppity air about her, as if she thought she was better than her other siblings. When she talked to my mother, she'd always talk down about everyone else. I think since her and my mother were really close in age, she always seemed to want my mom to do what she did. One of those things was to go visit this woman.

I asked my mother what a prophetess was and she said someone who could see into your life, your past and your future, without even knowing you. She could tell you things that you didn't know. Mom took me and my younger brother Matthew with her when she went to see that woman. I was so scared, I didn't want her to be able to see the things I had been doing. I just knew she would tell my mother exactly what I had done.

When we got there, it was at someone else's house. There were extra chairs brought in so we could all have a seat. We sat one on each side of my mother. When everyone was settled in the lady began to talk to the whole group. A lot of the women nodded at what she said and said "yes" and "amen". She spoke for a very long time, so long that the sun went down and they had to turn on the lights. I really didn't understand any of what she was saying.

Soon enough Matthew fell asleep. I started to get tired myself but I was trying to keep an eye on her. I wanted to make sure that she didn't look at me for too long, otherwise she would see. I didn't want her to see. Eventually, I fell asleep, I couldn't help it.

The next thing I knew all the women were crying and shouting and most of them were standing up. I was alarmed to see how close she was to us. She was coming from the left and touching each person and telling them things about themselves and what was going to happen in their lives.

She would get to my brother first, then Mom, and then me. Everyone seemed to be either happy about the news she gave them or happy that she had laid her hands on them. I just knew I wouldn't be either. She touched my brother and spoke to my mother about him. Mom began to cry. She touched my mother and she cried even harder.

I started to cry because my mother was crying, but also because I knew I'd be in trouble after this one. She laid hands on me and my heart felt like it would jump out of my chest. My eyes were on the floor, I just couldn't look at her. My tears made the lines on the tile floor look squiggly. She had placed her hands on each side of my face, they were warm.

"Oh," that was all she had said and she stayed silent for a while. My curiosity got the best of me and I looked up. She was smiling at me and when my eyes reached hers, her smile deepened. She had a very kind face and her smile was a genuine one. She didn't look at me in hatred. She looked at me as if she loved me so much, but she didn't even know who I was. She didn't seem to know what I had done either.

She spoke to my mother, but she was looking at me.

"This one is a very special child," she said, "What's her name?" My mother took my hand and she said, "Gabriel." At the mention of my name all she said was, "Mmh." But her eyes held so much feeling and, in that moment, looking into her eyes all I felt was love. I was encased by it, it was a very warm feeling, and I felt it all over.

Still looking at me she told my mother, "She is so special, this child. And she will go through so much in her life. You need to make sure that you stick by her and watch over her. She needs your love." She kissed my forehead, then placed her hand where she had kissed me, and she prayed over me. All the while, my mother squeezed my hand, and when I looked up at her she smiled at me and for the first time I felt my mother's love.

I left from that encounter with a very warm feeling inside of me. No one had ever said I was special in a good way before. No one had ever looked at me the way she had before. I think she saw the very things I was afraid she would see, but strangely, she saw them in a different way.

She told my mother exactly what I had wanted from her all along, I wanted to be close to her, I wanted her protection, and I wanted her love. I just could not articulate those things to her myself and they would not sound right coming from my mouth. I kept that lady's love and her words in my heart, and I keep them still. But maybe one day I would have forgotten them if my mother had been able to heed what the prophetess had said.

CHAPTER 6

CHRISTMAS TIME

When I started pre-K, everything was different. The children seemed strange to me. A lot of them never sat still, they just ran around giggling, happy, and always playing. On my first day, my mother brought me to school. She always wore these long, flowing skirts. That day when we walked in, I felt so uncomfortable being there that I hid in the folds of her skirt.

When the teacher came to greet us, Mom tried to push me out. I was holding on way too tight so she couldn't. They talked for a while, the teacher tried to coax me out, it wasn't happening. Mom tried to tell me I would have fun here and I should go, but I'd never been anywhere else but home and this was a very strange place.

My father would never allow this much noise to go on. The teacher and my mom talked a little longer, but this time I remember the conversation. They were discussing how to extract me from my mother's skirt. They had this talk right in front of me as if I wouldn't understand.

My mother sat down in a chair near the door so that I had to remove myself a bit, but I still held on. The teacher went away and came back with some toys. She sat them a little too far out of my reach. I knew what she was doing. She wanted me to let go. I was not going to be tricked into staying there.

So, I sat, staring at the toys and holding on to mom's skirt. Mom patted my shoulder and said, "Go on, you can play with the toys." The teacher had sat them in a line, and it seemed like the nicest toys were the furthest away. There was one that was close, and I figured I could snatch that one up fast enough to get back to my mom before she had a chance to take off. I tried it and I made it.

I played with it one-handed for a while. When I got tired of it, I dashed for another one. That's when Mom tried to convince me that I could let go and play with the toy, she'd still be sitting there. So, I let go, but then I scooted so that my back was still touching her. But she was right, she didn't move.

She kept encouraging me to go and play with the other toys, that she would be there, she wasn't going anywhere. I scooted out some to get some of the toys and looked back just to see if she was there. She smiled and told me to play, so I did. Each time I scooted to get another toy I'd look back and she was still there. Eventually, I got so engrossed in playing that I forgot to keep looking every now and then.

When I realized it, I whipped my head around, but she was gone. She had told me she would stay, but she didn't. I couldn't believe she'd left me there. I started to cry, and it took a very long time for the teacher to notice because I'd learned from my father not to cry out loud. So, there I sat, crying silently with my shirt and sleeves soaked with tears.

When she started to gather the children for another activity, I didn't move. I was frozen in place, still crying because my mother had left me, that's when she noticed me. She came over with a sad face and rubbed my back, it only made more tears fall. She tried to get me to sit in the circle, I didn't want to go. She tried telling me that my mom would be back later, that didn't work. She tried to get me to talk, I didn't say a word.

So, finally she gave me some tissue and left me there to cry. I don't remember going home, but I do remember mom bringing me back the next day and leaving me there. I sat and cried. I did not want to be here with these strange children who ran around making so much noise at times. This is not how things were at my house and all I wanted to do was go back home.

She eventually stopped giving me tissue and told me that I had to ask for it. It took me a few days to get up the nerve for that. I knew her and my mother talked because, every time I came home my mom would tell me about the teacher, and how precious she thought I was because I was so quiet and it broke her heart that I would sit there and cry silently. She told my mother that I almost made her cry every day when I did get around to asking her for a tissue. It took me a while to adjust to pre-K.

Obviously, I didn't adjust enough because I spent two

years in kindergarten after that. Something about the teacher thinking I wasn't mature enough to pass, that I didn't socialize well. I remember my sister Reagan arguing with my mother because I had gotten all Ss on my report cards, which meant I learned everything satisfactorily so, she shouldn't let them hold me back.

I learned that it was ultimately mom's decision whether to hold me back or not. If she didn't reply they would automatically hold me back. She didn't reply. You see, if mom didn't want them to hold me back, she would have had to go to the school herself and have a meeting with the teacher. Mom didn't like going to school because they usually asked her to read something. Mom couldn't read and she was embarrassed about it. So, rather than admit it, she just wouldn't show up.

First grade ran pretty much the same; except there was no more crying. I still wouldn't talk to anyone besides one girl, I considered her my best friend. By the second time I was in first grade they were under the impression that I had some kind of speech problem. Again, I was still making straight As in everything; I just wouldn't talk to the teacher or the other students. The only time I talked was at recess with my best friend.

They decided to send me to speech class in my second year of first grade. I loved that class. All you did was sit and draw and color, it was fun. The teacher would come and sit with you just to chat from time to time, that was nice too. A lot of the other kids sounded strange when they spoke, but they were nice and quiet and there weren't many of them. This was a nice class.

The teacher would come and sit at my table and talk to me for a while each day. We'd have conversations about a lot of different things. It was nice to talk to her. I was in her class for about a week or two and then she told me I couldn't come there any longer. I asked her why; she said it was because there was nothing wrong with my speech. She said that she could tell that I was very smart and she didn't understand why they would put me in her class.

The next day I was back in my normal classroom all day and I never went to her class again. I missed going there a lot. I remember that I used to stop by sometimes and ask if I could come back. She'd always tell me no, but that she did miss me. I just couldn't understand why if she missed me, she wouldn't take me back.

From being in school I learned a lot of things. One important thing was that there was a Santa Clause. The sad part about that is he never visited my house. Every year around Christmas time the kids at school would talk about Santa and what he was going to get them for Christmas. The teachers would make us write letters to Santa and make Christmas lists during arts and crafts to take home to our parents. I hated those times.

Santa Clause never visited our house. My mom never made him cookies and milk. At first, I used to think that was why he never came. We had a chimney, just like the books said. But we didn't have cookies and milk and we never had a Christmas tree.

One day I mentioned Santa to Daniel and Derrick and they told me he wasn't real. For reassurance, I went to ask Reagan because she knew everything. She told me the truth, that Santa wasn't real. People just made up stories about him and it was really your parents who bought the Christmas presents and put them under the tree. She said that we didn't have Christmas because of Daddy.

So, every year I'd have to go through making a list of things I wanted and writing a letter to this man that didn't exist. It was fun at first, even knowing that it wasn't real. I'd pretend that there really was a Santa and that I'd get everything I wrote down on my Christmas list. It was all fun up until the day Christmas came and I'd come downstairs to see that there wasn't a tree stuffed with presents underneath.

We would go outside on Christmas day and watch other kids ride their brand-new bikes and play with their remote-controlled cars. Sometimes it was nice because they'd let us play with their new toys. But we'd always have to go home where there were no toys and no Christmas cheer. The only fun we had inside the house was watching the movies that came on every year.

Then one year, my oldest sister Marie was 18 or 19, and she had a very nice boyfriend. They got us a nice little Christmas tree and she told us to give her our Christmas lists. We were so ecstatic to have a tree with real lights on it inside the house. I took the time to think about what I really wanted that year. I remember writing down marbles, a Tonka Truck, a remote-controlled car. I was so excited. I just knew I'd get at least one thing on my list.

Presents began to show up under the tree. We were told not to touch them, but me and my brothers got needles from my mom's sewing kit and tried to poke small holes in the boxes to see what they were. It never worked. There was at least one box under there with my name on it. I couldn't wait until Christmas.

When the day rolled around, I rushed downstairs very early in the morning to find that everyone else had done the same. We were all so excited. We got to open our presents one by one. When it was my turn, I ripped the wrapping off the box and stopped in shock. It was a Barbie doll.

I couldn't believe it. Nowhere on my list had I written that I wanted a doll. I was so disappointed. Rachel noticed and proceeded to tell me that Marie could take it back to the store if I didn't like it and get her money back, then I would have nothing. I said no, lied and said that I liked it, then I sat to watch everyone else that was left.

CHAPTER 7

KEN AND BARBIE

My baby sister Karen had Godparents and every year they bought her loads of clothes and toys. So, we all sat to watch her open all her gifts. She was five years younger than me and every year it was like that. When she got old enough to realize it, she would tease me all day for Christmas because she had way more toys and things and every year, no matter what I put on my list, all I got was a doll or a purse. One year I even got an Easy Bake Oven.

They were things I never played with unless it was to decapitate Barbie, or cut off all her hair, or take her limbs and mix them around so that her arms became her legs and vice versa. Then there was one year when I got a Ken doll along with Barbie. Then things got interesting because I'd make Ken and Barbie have sex all the time. They'd always end up having this big, huge baby that didn't fit with their proportions because that's all I had.

Admittedly, I would get aroused when I made Ken play with Barbie. That was probably my best present back then. I'd always go off by myself and play with Ken and Barbie because I couldn't go outside. I'd come up with all different kinds of scenarios and they would all end in Ken and Barbie having sex. Then I'd end up masturbating.

It was my best friend back in those days. I would masturbate all the time. That's how I spent my days of boredom. I'd go off and either play with the dolls or come up with something in my own mind. Sometimes I used to think about hunching with Tommy. Other times I'd just get one of my little sister's teddy bears and hunch its leg until I came.

One day I did it right there in front of her because mom left her upstairs with me while she went to cook. Later on that day, she told my mom that I was doing nasty stuff to her teddy bear. I swung around in fear of what my mother would do. I thought for sure she would tell my father. But she was putting food on plates for dinner and all she said was, "Uh huh." She wasn't paying attention that day, so I decided that I'd have to be more careful.

When I was around eight years old mom started babysitting a little girl who was about six. I believe she was Rachel's boyfriend's daughter. She'd follow me everywhere and I didn't like it because I'd want to go off and masturbate and I couldn't. So, one day I was playing with my dolls and I didn't care whether she saw or not. She decided she wanted to play with me, so I let her.

When I got to the part where it was time for Ken and Barbie to have sex, she played right along with it. Of course, I was Ken and she was Barbie and I was amazed that she knew what to do. When it came time for me to masturbate, she wanted to lay under me and let me do it on her and I did.

This was new and exciting to me. We were both girls so no one ever came to check and see what we were doing. We spent a lot of time off by ourselves together. The only thing about her was that she would always end up wanting to play something else that I didn't want to play afterward, some dumb, girly game. I'd always say no, but then she'd threaten to tell on me if I didn't. That was truly my first love/hate friendship.

I liked what we did together, but I didn't like that she could back me into a corner. I couldn't describe what it was then, but I know now that she was very manipulative. I'd always fall into her trap and then I'd hate myself for it afterward because she'd outsmart me. I didn't like that she was younger but she knew more than I did in a sneaky kind of way, a way that I couldn't explain.

Every time she came over I would tell her that I don't want to play with her, but then she'd do something to get me aroused. She'd start the nasty play with my dolls on her own and I'd give up and join in and then later she'd use what I'd done as leverage to make me play her games.

One time I hid my dolls so she couldn't find them and did other stuff with my mom all day. I'd shown her who was boss. Then the next day she came with her own dolls and they were newer than mine so I ended up playing with her anyway and the cycle continued.

After a while I just gave up and hunched her and then played how she wanted to play. Then she flipped the routine on me and said we couldn't hunch until we played her games first. Sometimes I just hated her because she made me feel so stupid, like I couldn't think faster than her. Eventually, my mom stopped babysitting her and then I really did miss her because I was stuck in the house all by myself again.

CHAPTER 8

RACHEL

Previously, I mentioned that I thought I was going to be named the culprit in the incident where Matthew caught an STD. I had never mentioned any abuse where he was involved because the sexual abuse that Matthew and I received was totally separate from what happened with Daniel and Derrick. This abuse came by way of our sister, Rachel, who happens to be nine years older than me.

Almost every sibling in my family has bad stories to tell about Rachel. To my mother's chagrin, some of us have dubbed her "The Evil One".

It started when I was about four, at least that's as far back as I can remember it happening. Matthew and I were so close in age that we used to be bathed together. I don't know how long we had been bathing together, but I don't remember noticing that he was different until Rachel pointed it out one day during bath time.

She had told me to look at him and look at myself and tell her what was different. I was confused because I had no clue what she was talking about. Anything I had ever experienced before this did not involve me seeing a penis.

After a short while, she seemed a bit exasperated, like I should know what she was talking about. She was always like that. She'd ask a question or tell you to do something that wasn't quite clear to you and get angry because you didn't have an answer. I felt like she always left things out on purpose.

She then proceeded to point out his penis and then show me on my own body that I didn't have one, that I had a hole down there instead. When I realized what she was saying and agreed that we were different she told me to touch his penis. I remember putting a finger out to poke it.

She slapped my hand and told me, "Not like that!" And then she told me to grab it with my whole hand. That's all I remember from that bath time. She had made me very nervous and scared because if I didn't do exactly what she wanted me to, as if I knew how she wanted me to touch something, she would get angry and hit me.

Things like that happened every time she bathed us. She would tell me to do something and if I got it wrong, she would hit me, then she would go into detail as to how I should do it the right way. I used to wish that she would tell me from the start exactly how she wanted me to do something so I could avoid getting hit. Even when I wasn't sure and I would ask her she would hit me and tell me to just shut up and do it.

When I had gotten used to what she wanted us to do she stopped hitting me. She would just tell us to do it while she watched. She would always just sit there and watch. Then one day we were getting a bath by two of our other older sisters. I want to say one was Reagan and I don't remember who the other one was, maybe Samantha or Marie.

That day I reached out and touched Matthew's penis and they were shocked. I remember one leaving the room to call mom while the other one stayed. Mom just came in and told them to take us out of the bath. I didn't really know what they were all so shocked about. I just remember them drying us off and mom saying that we could no longer take a bath together.

After that I missed taking baths with Matthew. Not because of what Rachel made us do, but because when she wasn't the one bathing us, we used to splash and play while we were being bathed. I didn't have him to play with anymore and it wasn't fun taking a bath alone.

Even after that, Rachel found other ways to get us alone. I remember being upstairs in her room and that's when she taught us how to hunch on each other with our pants down. She liked to see our private areas touching when we did it. That's where I picked up the habit of hunching without clothes separating us.

I don't really know for what span of time she had us doing things together, but I know it was when I was very young. By the time I was about six I don't remember anymore of her making Matthew and I do things while she watched. That's not the only thing that happened because of her, though. That wasn't the only reason why I was afraid of her.

When I was around six, I used to sleep in the bed with Reagan. The problem there was that I was a very bad sleeper. We'd go to sleep on the same side of the bed, but before the night was over, I'd end up kicking her or my foot would end up in her mouth or some other inappropriate place.

She used to complain about it all the time. Mom never did anything about it so she started kicking me out of the bed when I would cause her discomfort in my sleep. I'd end up on the floor under the bed by morning, never realizing how I got there because I would never wake up when she kicked me.

Well, one night I did wake up during the kicking process and it hurt when I landed on the floor. I began to cry loudly. From that night on Mom said I had to sleep with Rachel instead of Reagan. I believe it was because Rachel had a bigger bed. That's when things started to happen to me in my sleep. Some things I'm not sure if I suffered from by her hands or not.

One thing that I do remember is the physical abuse. I wouldn't know if I had done something to Rachel or not. I just remember being punched, pinched, and kicked out of my sleep. Whatever she did to me it always hurt badly. I know because Reagan had kicked me out of the bed almost every night for a while before I woke up that one time. With Rachel, I always woke up.

I'd end up silently crying a lot during those nights sleeping with Rachel. Sometimes she would punch me in my stomach so hard that I'd wake up fighting for breath. Or when

48

she'd pinch me out of my sleep she wouldn't stop when I woke up, she would continue to twist my skin and I could feel her nails digging in.

I would always be afraid to go to sleep. I'd lay there on the very edge of the bed with my eyes wide open, willing myself to stay awake, but every night I'd fall asleep and then she would do something painful to wake me out of my sleep. I don't recall whether I had kicked her or not while sleeping. I just remember so many nights laying at the edge of that bed crying.

Rachel was also very good at doing hair at a young age. So, she would always braid my hair and my mom also trusted her to straighten my hair. It was the straightening that scared me the most about her.

To straighten my hair without using chemicals you had to use a straightening comb. Back then, it wasn't the kind that you plugged into the wall. This ironing comb was a heavy iron comb with a black handle. You would set the iron part of the comb on the eye of the stove where the heat came from.

When it was hot enough, which meant hot enough to burn skin, it was then picked up by its black handle and combed through the hair. It would have to get as close to the natural roots of the hair as possible without touching the scalp and then combed outward. This was done to straighten the coarse roots of my hair.

To get that close without the heat itself burning the

scalp, the person combing through the hair would have to use their mouth to blow air onto the area where the comb was closest. That way it would blow the heat away from the scalp. The problem with that was sometimes Rachel wouldn't do this.

She would always hit me if I flinched when she'd put the hot comb in my hair. But, if no one was around to watch, she wouldn't blow on my scalp so I would flinch away from the heat and she would hit me. Sometimes she'd warn me not to move or else, but during the warning she'd be swinging the comb extremely close to my body. Then she would put the comb in my hair with a gleam in her eyes, as if she were anticipating that I would flinch. You could tell that she enjoyed torturing me.

My mom would always compliment her on how well she would do my hair. I always had naturally thick, coarse hair and when she would braid it people would ask if my hair was a weave because it was so thick. I think my mother was proud of the thickness of my hair. Even though Rachel's hair was as thick as mine, I don't think she liked that my hair was like hers and that my mother seemed to be proud of it.

So, one day while mom was gone Rachel decided to hot comb my hair. She did what she would always do to torture me, but this time she seemed extra giddy about it. I went through the whole ordeal wondering why she was so happy. My oldest sister came out to the living room and yelled Rachel's name and asked why she smelled burnt hair.

Marie, who came over in concern, was thirteen years

older than me and four years older than Rachel. I started panicking when she started fussing at Rachel and telling her that mom would be angry when she came home. Rachel kept saying she hadn't been paying attention and she didn't know that she had done it. I didn't know what "it" was, I was not allowed to get out of the chair until mom came home. I believe that Marie thought Rachel had known exactly what she was doing and that she had done it on purpose.

When mom came home, she was highly upset when she saw my hair. Both Rachel and Marie were yelling over each other trying to tell mom their different versions of the story. But Rachel was always a very good liar and she could be extremely convincing when she thought she might be in trouble. As always, mom believed Rachel when she said it was an accident.

They took a while looking over my hair and Rachel told mom that she would personally take care of my hair for a while until it grew back. When I was finally let down off the chair I went straight to the bathroom. Though I still had some hair on the sides of the front of my head, a good bit of it had fallen out from the heat. It was very thin on each side to the point that you could see my scalp.

As thick as my hair was, you could never see my scalp unless my hair was braided down to it. I never much cared about my hair until that day. I stood there looking in the mirror and crying. Rachel walked in and smiled. She came up behind me and put a hand on my shoulder. She looked at me through the mirror, chuckled a little and said, "It'll grow back." Then she walked away with a bounce in her step as if she didn't have a care in the world.

She kept her word and took care of my hair until it grew back. She kept it braided, no more hot combs for a long time and I was glad of that. But the sides of my hair were never the same. It grew back, but never as thick as the rest of my hair. I think Rachel was happy about the outcome of that.

As I got older her ways of torturing became less physical and more like a mental game she played. It was a game of manipulation. When I was old enough, she started sending me on errands throughout the house. All of them ended in me going to fetch her something that she didn't feel like getting up to get herself. It was an all day, everyday process for me.

I'd get tired of doing things for her and she'd start to notice because I'd let out a long sigh when she would ask me to go get something else. When she'd notice, she would always tell me that I didn't have to do it if I didn't want to. She would always be so nice about it and say it was my choice whether I felt like doing it or not.

And the minute I'd tell her I didn't feel like doing something she would get someone else to do it and give them something for doing it. It would always be something I would have really wanted, like candy or a quarter or something. You could get a lot of candy with a quarter back in the 80s. Then she would tell me that, had I gone and done it for her I could've gotten something for it. So, the next time she would ask me if I wanted to go get something for her I would hop to it.

I was always eager to do it after that because I thought that one day she'd give me something for fetching things for her. I'd go run errands for her for a month or two, it would seem. But she would never give me anything for it. Eventually, my patience would run thin again and we'd go through that whole process over and over again.

After going through this for a while with her I'd begun to get angry at the unfairness of it all. I was the one who went and got most of the things she asked for, but she never gave me anything for it. I tried to mask my anger about it all, but she was very good at reading people or maybe I wasn't very good at hiding my emotions. She would ask if I was angry or something with a smile on her face and I'd always tell her no, but she knew better.

One day she sent me upstairs to go and get something out of her top drawer. When I went up there and opened the drawer she had a wad of money in it. It was a lot of money to me. I'd never seen so much money just sitting there. I stared at it for a minute. I thought to myself that this would be the perfect time to take what she owed me.

All that time I had spent running around and doing things for her, I deserved something for all my hard work. So, I did what I thought was the smart thing. I took a little bit of the money, but not all of it. I left most of it there and figured she wouldn't notice a few dollars missing and, by the time she did, I would have spent it all. I took the money and tucked it in my underwear.

When I went back downstairs with what she had told me to get, she looked at me suspiciously and asked why it had taken me so long. I didn't think it had taken me long at all, but I lied and told her it had taken me a minute to find it. She looked me straight in the eye with that gleam in hers and asked me point blank if I had taken some of her money.

Nervously, I told her no. She smiled and said, "Fine, then you won't mind me searching you." What she did next was a surprise. She pulled me closer to her and her hand went straight into my underwear, exactly where I had placed the money. When she found it, she continued to smile and said, "I thought you said you didn't take my money?"

I opened my mouth, but I really had nothing to say. That's when her face changed, like night and day. She looked at me with what looked like hate and said, "You ain't nothing but a thief!" And she proceeded to tell all my siblings who were around her that I was a thief. She even got some of them to call me a thief.

She, along with them, were chanting the word thief at me until I started to cry. For a very long time after that she wouldn't call me by my name, she'd call me "thief" instead, as if it were my name. She didn't send me to run errands for a while after that either.

I felt so bad for a long time. She made me feel like I was the worst kind of person. I wanted so much to be back in her good graces. Finally, one day she asked me to do something for her and she stressed the point that she hoped I wouldn't steal from her when I went to fetch whatever it was that she wanted. She said it very meanly, too. I promised her that I wouldn't and I didn't.

That day she stopped calling me "thief" and started calling me by my name again. After that, out of fear, I always ran errands for her. I never complained about it again. I never sighed in front of her. I never let her know that I was tired of doing anything she asked me to do. And from then on out, just like before, she never gave me anything for doing as she asked.

CHAPTER 9

MISSING BUSES

I used to love to go to the store with my mother. Sometimes I didn't get to go because, before my dad banned me from going outside, I was always dirty. My mother tirelessly kept everything clean. Everything! I was the total opposite of everything clean, neat, and orderly. She would constantly complain about me being dirty, ashy, and barefooted. I was never allowed to go to the grocery store with her looking like that.

I remember it well. I would hear dad's truck start up and I'd come running to see if it was my mother. I'd chase after the truck yelling that I wanted to go. She'd always stop, look me over, then say I couldn't go with her because I was dirty and she'd pull off with the rest of my sisters in tow. I'd be so sad that I couldn't go.

Even though we couldn't get any sweets or anything aside from what was on her list of things to get, I'd want to go just to look at all the sweets and cool cereals and things that we never got to have. Mom always bought the cheapest things she could. She'd have to make the money stretch because dad never gave her much. I always felt like she bought mostly beans because they were the cheapest. When we ran out of other foods, she'd always have her trusty beans and rice handy.

Dad never gave mom enough money for food. He worked a lot and I always saw that my dad had a lot of money, but he didn't spend a lot of it on us. My dad always kept beer in the fridge, but he still went out to the bar a lot. I'd hear stories about how dad had bought drinks for everyone in the bar. My oldest siblings, especially Marie, would talk about how she'd seen daddy with one woman or another.

She'd end up telling Mom, but when Mom would confront Dad about it he would deny it and my mom seemed to believe him. She'd go back into her normal routine like she didn't have a doubt in her mind that he was telling the truth.

When I did get to go to the store the only sweets she'd ever pick up were for my father. She'd put a snack cake in his lunch every day when he went to work. When he'd come back home, we couldn't wait until he put his lunch box down and go into their bedroom. Everyone would race to his lunchbox and whoever got there first would usually get whatever he had left in there. If he did leave something, it was often the snack cake.

Sometimes mom used to go to the store with all ten of us trailing behind her. People would always compliment her on how quiet and well behaved we were. They'd look on in awe because we would never beg her for anything, unlike their own children. But we knew never to ask mom for something that wasn't on her list. If we did she would tell our father and we would get a whipping for it.

That's always how my mother kept us in line. We would never do anything she disliked for fear of our father. I would always try my best not to do anything that she would have to report back to him.

Once, I remember taking too long to get dressed for school and as I was walking out the front door the bus was closing its doors and pulling off. I couldn't go back inside because then I'd end up staying home and she'd tell my father when he got home from work.

So, I turned around and ran behind the house. The projects were directly behind our house and right on the other side of the projects was the elementary school. I thought that if I cut straight through the projects I could make it to school on time. With that plan in mind, I ran as fast as I could.

I was so afraid that I wouldn't make it there on time. I was also afraid that the school would call my mother if I made it there late and I would have run for nothing. With fear in my heart working against its proper function I was losing breath very quickly.

Then suddenly I heard growling and barking behind me. As I looked behind me to see what it was, my feet continued to pound the ground. To my devastation, it was indeed a dog. I was always taught not to run from dogs, but there was no time to stop and the chase added to my fears because this was no ordinary, innocent looking, tongue lolling dog. This was a Rottweiler and he looked vicious.

On top of that, up ahead was a fence. That fence had to be at least three feet tall. He was gaining on me very quickly so, if I tried to run around the fence he would have me before I ever made it to the corner of it. There was nothing left to do but try to jump it. When I did, I was amazed that my entire body made it over without even touching it. The same occurred when I jumped the other side to get out of the yard.

To my relief, the dog didn't realize that if he ran around the fence he could catch up with me. Instead he kept jumping up trying to make it over the first side of the fence that I had hopped. By this time, I felt like my heart was going to beat out of my chest, but I kept going.

When I reached the school, I ran around the front to the side where the bus lanes were. To my disappointment, there were no buses there. I just knew for sure that I was going to get it then. I had no more breath in me and as tears welled up in my eyes I had to put my hands on my knees. I was so out of breath I felt as if I would fall over and my heart would burst out of my chest. All I felt was pain in my chest as I tried to breathe, sucking air into my lungs loudly with no relief.

I was breathing so hard that I didn't hear the buses until they were pulling into the bus lane. One by one I watched them in confusion as teachers began filing out of the hallways to the bus lane to escort children inside. There's no way I could've made it on time, was my thought.

But sure enough, my bus pulled in and stopped directly in front of me. I could see my brothers' faces as they looked at me, amazed. I leaned against a pole in relief, tears flowing down my face. Not only had I made it, but I had beaten the bus to school. Fear can make you do things you never thought you were capable of.

I watched them as the bus door opened. They seemed to be pushing against the other children trying to get off the bus. Once free, they immediately ran to where I was, still trying to catch my breath. They came with a barrage of questions, none of which I could answer right off because I still could not catch my breath.

When I explained everything to them they looked on in disbelief. To them, there was no way that I could've beaten the bus to school; someone must have dropped me off. But when they took in the tears and my efforts even still to try and catch my breath, there was nothing else to do but believe me.

They, all three of them, had been afraid for me. Daniel and Derrick each took one of my arms and put them over their shoulders to help me as Matthew led the way to the cafeteria for breakfast. After that, I tried my best to make sure I never missed another bus.

Until one afternoon, I don't remember why I had missed the bus home, but I remember walking very slowly because I dreaded what would happen when I got there. I was right at the beginning of the projects, school side, when I heard someone say, "Which child are you?"

I looked over and saw that it was my Auntie Connie, my father's sister. We didn't visit her very often and as a child all the buildings in the projects looked the same so I never knew which one she lived in.

Aunt Connie was in a wheelchair and she was missing a leg. She was nothing like my father and when my mother brought us to visit her she was always nice to us. I smiled and ran over to her. She greeted me warmly, as always, and I told her which number I was and my name.

She told me to come inside, but I remembered that I had missed the bus and I told her I was afraid to go home. When she asked why I told her. Her remarks made my reason sound like utter nonsense. She then proceeded to call my house and tell my father that I was there with her, that I'd be home soon, and that he'd better not lay a hand on me for being there.

I was amazed that she would talk to my father in such a way. I was also surprised that she hung up the phone as if all was well. Then she went into her room, rummaged around in a drawer and pulled out some money. She sent me to the store down the street with specific instructions on what kind of sweets to get her and she gave me a dollar to buy myself something. I was so excited but also anxious at what awaited me when I got home.

I went to the store, like she asked. She was very pleased that I came back with precisely what she asked me to get and that I'd given her more change back than she'd expected. I thought, since she was so nice, I should only get a honey bun for twenty-five cents. I spoke with her for a few more minutes and then I left to go home. When I got there my father didn't even acknowledge my presence. He just went about the rest of his day like normal.

After that I started to walk home often and stop by to see her. She was always happy to see me and we would talk for a while, then she'd send me to the store and I would go home afterwards. One day I told her about a whipping I had gotten for no reason. She seemed very angry about it.

When I got home that day my father wasn't there so I didn't think anything of it. The next day when I stopped at her house my father was there, standing outside waiting for me. Auntie Connie wasn't sitting inside the screen door waiting as she usually does. Her front door was closed.

My father's face turned to hatred and he grabbed me roughly by the arm and shoved me in the truck. When we got home he whipped me until I urinated on myself, except this time, he didn't walk away in disgust. He got even angrier about it and beat me even more.

I remember the welts stinging from the soap suds when I very carefully took a bath that evening. He didn't say much after the whipping other than I was never allowed to walk home or go over to Auntie Connie's house alone again. I don't remember seeing her much after that, but when I did see her again the first thing she asked was why I stopped coming over. I gave her some noncommittal answer and left it at that. She looked at me sadly, but she never mentioned it again.

* H a r d   T i m e s

What have I ever done to make you be so mean to me?

I don't mean to be so disgusting to your sensibility

To you, I am not worth the price of a grain of rice

To you, I am not sugar and spice and you're not nice

You're not the father that says, "sweet dreams" to me at night

You're the nightmare in the closet that growls, out of sight

Out of mind, out of my mind, I wish I could blot you out

I wish I could turn back time and make sense of all the doubt

All the scars, all the whippings, the name-calling, disgusted stares

The looks that said to me so clearly that you don't care

But I guess you do care, I mean to say that you hate

Because you give attention to me I wish would dissipate

Disappear, I'd like to do if I had a magic power

Instead I think up ways that you could die so tragic, Hours

Of time I spend daydreaming about a life with no blues

With no whippings, no fears, no tears, no hate, and no you

CHAPTER 10

ALL ABOUT BIKES

When I turned five my father thought it high time that I learned how to ride a bike. To my horror, he decided to be the one that was going to teach me. The whole family came outside to watch this. Even the neighbors across the street were outside and moved their vehicles out of the way after I had run into one of them.

No matter how many times my dad tried to get me to ride steady, I just couldn't do it. I was too afraid of him to concentrate on balancing properly or anything else he said. Added to that was the fear that if I failed I would get a whipping. He finally gave up after about an hour of riding but said that we'd try again the next day when he came home from work.

That put me on edge and I didn't sleep well at all that night. The next day when we tried again I still couldn't concentrate on what he was telling me and the more frustrated he got the worse my riding became. As soon as he let go I fell immediately, every single time. After that day, he quit trying and my brothers started to tease me because I couldn't ride a bike.

One day that summer I got angry about it and while they were off playing, I took the one bike that we all shared and went out into the street with a determination that I was going to learn. The neighbor's wife came out as soon as she saw me and moved her car. I ignored it, I had my mind set that today I wouldn't run into anything and that I was going to conquer this.

I tried repeatedly and it took me a while, but I finally got the hang of it. I remember my jumps of victory. I was still a bit wobbly with it, but I was excited to show my brothers that I had taught myself. When they came home I was going to be all up in their faces, and I was.

From then on out I was all about bikes. I'd be right there with my brothers when they were fixing our bike. I was always excited when one of our friends got himself a new bike. We'd all take a turn riding it. I never liked the girl's bikes with their U-shaped handlebars, pink and purple colors, and glitter all over the place with the little white baskets in the front. No, the boys always had cooler bikes.

So, one day I decided that I would buy one of those cool bikes for myself. My grandma, my father's mother, lived with us and she would always give us two dollars a month. Before, I couldn't wait to get it and it was always gone as soon as she placed it in my hands. I always spent it on junk food. I was like a crack fiend when it came to junk food because my mother never bought any for us.

But then I started to want a bike more than I wanted junk food. So, every month I'd save my two dollars and put it away in a sock in my drawer. I'd find money on the ground; I'd do things for my older siblings for some change. Any way I could make money, I would. Within about six or seven months I had about twenty-four dollars.

It was very tempting having that much money because there were so many things I could buy with it that weren't as much as a bike. I remember thinking of all the junk food I could get with that much money, but I kept my resolve. I was half way to my goal of owning my own brand-new bike!

Then one day after school I had gone to check on my money. I was so nervous to have that much money, I'd always check on it as soon as I came in from school. I looked in the drawer and my money was nowhere to be found. In a panic, I started to cry and ran downstairs to tell my mother.

She was cooking when I told her and she turned around angrily, swinging the spoon. She told me that she found that money in my drawer and was wondering how I had gotten it. I told her that I had been saving it for months. When she asked for what, I told her.

I asked her if I could have it back and she told me no. She said that we needed food in the house and she seemed very angry that I would save money to buy a stupid bike. So, she kept the money and told me she had better plans for it. She told me she was going to show me what I should be spending money on.

She took me with her the next time she went to the store and bought groceries and I watched in tears as she took all the money I had saved up and counted it out to the cashier. All that time I had spent thinking about bikes, picking out bikes when I went to the store with her, pricing the bikes, and counting my change up to see how much I had left to reach my goal. I was so angry with my mother, helplessly, hopelessly angry.

I felt like she had betrayed me, as usual. I felt like she had literally stolen my money and didn't care one bit that she had taken it. Taken it away and spent it on something that was supposedly more important than anything I could ever think of buying.

After that I was either stuck with taking turns with the one bike we had or riding our friends' bikes because ours had gotten stolen again. Every time we got a bike it was only a matter of time before it got stolen. One bike, and it was as if the kids from the projects were waiting on us to slip up. As soon as they got the chance they'd steal it and spray paint it all one color so that it was unrecognizable.

Once when it had gotten stolen Daniel found it at the corner store. He had known it was ours because he'd scratched a mark into the frame that was visible even under the black spray paint. He'd run home to tell us and Reagan fussed at him for not taking it right then.

Derrick, Reagan, and I quickly ran back to the store with him and grabbed the bike. We all walked home laughing that day because we'd found our bike again.

. . .

I always played with Daniel, Derrick, and their friends.

Some of their friends had sisters my age but they always wanted to play girlie games that I was never interested in. I did everything they did. I wrestled, played marbles, and tried to play basketball with them. I'd always get aggravated and sit down because I couldn't dribble well and they'd always steal the ball from me before I could make a shot.

Whatever they were doing, I was into it. Especially when they started to learn bike tricks. I learned how to ride with no hands, stand on the seat and coast, pop a wheelie, and skid on gravel; that was my favorite.

After a while, one of their friends showed us how to break with your foot instead of using the pedals. They'd ride hard and then stand with one foot on the pedals and place the other on the back tire hard so that the bike would skid to a stop.

I thought it was the coolest thing yet and I just had to try it. So, I got on the friend's bike, gained up enough speed, and lifted my foot to stop the back wheel. Even as I was doing it I heard them all screaming for me not to, but my attitude was that I'd show them. I thought that they were yelling because they didn't think that I could do it. Whenever they would tell me I couldn't I would always prove them wrong, it was ingrained in me to show them up and shut them up.

But, oh no, this time they were telling me not to for a reason. I didn't have any shoes on. I always ran around barefoot and it didn't occur to me that all of them had done this with shoes on. So, when my right foot hit the tire it immediately slammed it into the frame behind the seat of the bike.

From there my foot slipped off the frame and my toes got caught inside the spokes. As the wheel turned, my foot hit the bottom part of the frame that was also attached to the wheel. Since it could go no further, my toes suffered.

They had gotten twisted around in the spokes and because the wheel was still turning and my foot was immobile, what happened next was horrifying. All I felt was tearing and pain and then I finally fell off the bike. The neighbor across the street from us was screaming. She ran off her porch and up to the end of the driveway, but would go no further.

She instructed one of my brothers to go to me and another to go and get my mother. We had all forgotten for a second that Mom wasn't home. She had left and taken everyone with her except for Daniel, Derrick, Matthew, and me. I got left for the usual reasons.

We were all afraid at this point. For fear of my father, the friend and his bike were long gone. No one wanted to go inside, least of all me. He was there, sitting in the living room watching the news. Something he always did at this time of day. And every single one of us knew never to disturb my father when he was watching television, especially the news.

At this point, though, we had no choice. The neighbor was instructing Daniel to help me inside so that our father could tend to me. We had to do as she said because it would have been ten times worse had she knocked on the door herself and told my father that we were being disobedient on top of me hurting myself.

So, to my amazement, Daniel picked me up. I didn't think he could do that. Even the neighbor was surprised. I wrapped my arms around his neck and began to cry. Not because of my foot, but because I was going to get a whipping all because mom wasn't home and we would interrupt his television show.

I hadn't seen my foot yet. I didn't want to look at it, but I did see the small puddle of blood where I had fallen to the ground and the trail of dots we were leaving behind. I was more worried about what my father would do than the condition of my foot. At that point, I didn't even feel the pain.

Daniel brought me inside through the sliding glass doors in the back. They opened into the dining room where he pulled out a chair and sat me in it, the chair closest to where my father was in the living room. He glanced over to where I sat, Daniel standing beside me. Derrick and Matthew stayed outside, afraid of what the consequence would be.

"What y'all done did now?" The question was asked calmly, but that never assuaged our fears. Father could always appear to be the calmest person before he broke into a rage. I couldn't find my voice so Daniel explained that my foot slipped off the pedal because I was riding so hard and my toes had gotten caught in the spokes. Of course, that was a lie, but it sounded a hell of a lot better than the truth.

My dad turned to look at me, shook his head and said, "Y'all chirren don't know what to git at." That meant that he was amazed at the things we could get ourselves into. Basically, what that meant to me was that I wasn't getting a whipping. I was so relieved and as I sat back and let out a long breath, so did Daniel. It seemed we'd both been holding it in.

Daniel then smiled at me and when I smiled back he quickly scurried out the door where I saw Derrick and Matthew worriedly waiting. When they saw Daniel's face they both began to smile and all three ran off happy and reassured. I sat smiling, relieved tears brimming at the edges of my eyelids.

Dad just sat there and continued to watch his news show. That made me even happier because it would have been far more nerve wracking if he had come over to look or, worse, tried to tend to it. Thankful that his attention was no longer on me, I finally looked at my foot.

Half of my foot, from the toes down, was blood red. I could still make out each individual toe and was relieved to see that none had broken off. The only problem was that all my toes had skin just hanging here and there off them making them look awfully mangled. But when I tried to wiggle my toes they all worked, nothing was broken, it just felt like I had wet sand between them.

I don't know how long I sat there, but by the time my mom came home there was a small puddle of blood beneath my foot and dad was still watching TV. My mom and sisters all gathered around for a few seconds and then mom began giving orders. Within minutes she had cleaned my foot and fussed at me about not being careful.

I was banned from riding bikes for some weeks. Within about two months everything was back to normal. All in all, I was just happy that I had not gotten a whipping.

CHAPTER 11

BRIEF ENCOUNTERS

I had so many different things going on with me sexually as a child. There were only three of my siblings that I had no sexual encounters with at all and they were Marie, Charlie, and Reagan. I don't remember much about Charlie at a very young age because he was never really there.

There's only a few things that I do remember. He worked with my father when he wasn't in school. Charlie was also extremely hot tempered and he and Marie got into fights that would scare me sometimes because he was strong enough to make her bleed. But she seemed to always get him back by kicking him in between his legs. Lastly, he was a lot like my father, so I steered clear of him.

Other than that, the only other persons I haven't mentioned are Samantha and Karen. I tried hunching Karen when she was about three or four, which would've made me around eight or nine. This was after the girl my mother babysat went away. Karen was not a very willing participant and she'd fuss about it. Then afterward she'd tell my mother and that scared the hell out of me. I only did it maybe two or three times, but then I left her alone.

Out of everything that happened to me sexually, I think I can be honest and say I had fun with Samantha. She'd always make it out to be like a game after that first time.

One day when I was upstairs playing alone she caught me making Ken hunch Barbie. She asked me what I knew about that and I just shrugged my shoulders. She then proceeded to lie on the floor on her back and told me to show her what I knew how to do. So, I did. I climbed on top of her and I hunched her until I climaxed.

When I was done, I stood up and looked at her warily. All she did was stand up, fix her clothes and said, "I just wanted to see how nasty you was." After that she just walked out without another word.

I don't remember much about Samantha in that respect. I just remember her making a game of it the few times that I do remember. She'd have us both lying on the floor in the same position and then she'd roll until she rolled on top of me. She'd hunch me a few times and then roll off. Then she'd wait for me to do the same thing to her.

We did this once with Reagan looking on in disgust. I remember her telling us that we were nasty and Samantha just laughed about it so I did too. Reagan seemed to be upset at this. I don't know if she had a private conversation with Samantha or not, but after that time Samantha never approached me again.

CHAPTER 12

THE BEGINNING OF THE SCARY END

Mom and Dad started arguing in their room on a regular basis. For years Marie had been telling my mother that we'd see my dad in his truck with another woman, but mom never really did anything about it. I don't know what made her start confronting him now, but that's what all their arguments were about.

I was ten years old at the time and it was my first time seeing that my mother wasn't happy. In all my childhood, I never really noticed how my mother felt because she didn't show much emotion. She never hugged us or told us that she loved us. I just always saw her cooking, cleaning, shopping at the grocery store, or watching her stories every day.

It was strange to see her looking sad and catching her crying from time to time. Every time they argued my father would end up leaving the house, always carrying a brown paper bag. When he would leave, my older siblings would either go into my parent's room or my mother would come out. Either way, she would be crying.

All I knew at the time is that my mom was certain that

my father was cheating. My three oldest siblings weren't living at home. Marie had moved out with her boyfriend and gotten married. Charlie had moved all the way to Georgia and I think Rachel either stayed with roommates or a boyfriend.

For whatever reason, Samantha wasn't there that day. So, from oldest to youngest it was Reagan, Daniel, Derrick, me, Matthew, and Karen at home. Out of the two of them, I would always side with my mother because regardless of her aloofness, she was the lesser threat. I would rather be ignored any day than whipped. Plus, my mother was very kind to other people. She was also very quiet and soft hearted. So, it always disturbed me when she cried. In my eyes, my father was always the bad guy and I hated him for making my mother cry.

One day after he left with his brown paper bag I asked my mother what was in it. She told me that it was his gun. See, every now and then I'd see my dad come in or leave with a paper bag, but now I saw that bag all the time so it triggered my curiosity. When I asked her why he carried it, she told me it was because he was afraid that we were going to do something to him. She told me that he was afraid of his own children.

That made absolutely no sense to me. My father had beaten me from as far back as I could remember. Why in the world would he be afraid of us? But, one day, I found out the answer.

He and my mother were arguing in their room one afternoon and he started getting loud, he sounded very enraged. From his yelling, I gathered that my mother had told him she was going to leave him. I never heard my mother's side of the conversation, only his. Whenever they argued their door was always locked. I know because Reagan had tried to get in before.

After a few minutes more of them heatedly arguing, Mom angrily left their bedroom. Dad, walking quickly behind her, basically chest bumped her into our bathroom. He then proceeded to tell her that she couldn't go anywhere if he shot her dead. Clear as day he told her that he would kill her. I was shocked and very afraid for my mother.

When Reagan heard him say that he would kill our mother, she ran into the kitchen and began to collect things and hand them out to each one of us. I was so scared that this was going to be the end for all of us. That my father would shoot my mother and then come out and shoot all of us because we were all brandishing bats, pots, and knives.

Reagan was always the brave one in my eyes. She hated my father, the same as we all did, but the difference was that she'd look him dead in his eyes where he could see it. She was fifteen years old at the time of this argument, but her age nor stature didn't matter when up against my father.

Reagan had the biggest cast iron skillet and she stood us all in a line in the hallway. She had us facing our bathroom and she was first in line. She was the only one that had no trace of fear on her face. That alone gave me strength enough to even hold the weapon she'd given me.

At this moment, Reagan slammed the bathroom door open and said very sternly, "Is there a problem?"

When Reagan slammed the door open, my father had the gun to Mom's head. He didn't say a word, he just stood there watching us. When he finally collected himself, he lowered the gun to his side. "And what y'all gon do!?!" he said boldly, but still looking a bit shaken.

"If you hurt our momma, we gon kill you!" This coming from Reagan, just as loud as my father, except she looked far more determined than shaken. He stood there for a moment and looked at each one of us and our weapons, and then he grunted, shook his head and walked away, right out the front door.

After Dad left, Reagan went to check and make sure he was gone. She was concerned that he might double back to do us harm. When we went in to check on Mom, she was still very angry. Reagan, ever the one to take action, hugged my mother and told her that we needed to leave.

I don't know the details of it all, but somehow my mother ended up on the phone with Charlie who was very irate and threatening to drive down to confront our father. This would not be good because, with Charlie's temper, someone would end up dead or seriously hurt. And, knowing my father, it would most likely be Charlie.

But somehow, Marie and Rachel became aware of the situation. It was decided that they, along with their husband and boyfriend, would drive us all up to Georgia to live with Charlie. This was all new, scary, and exciting all at one time.

To my knowledge, I had never been more than an hour outside of the small town we lived in. It only took about forty-five minutes to get to Baton Rouge and that's as far as I'd ever been.

Over a few days everything was planned. We were all given a large black trash bag and told to fill it with only our clothes and things that were important. There wasn't much room to pack things because of the number of people going. So, at the end of April 1992, my mother left my father and moved to Georgia.

I remember her crying off and on all the way there. I started to cry too, but for a different reason. The road that we were on was called the interstate and it had a huge wall dividing it from the traffic on the other side. Somehow, we missed an exit that we were supposed to take while following Rachel and her boyfriend.

All I was aware of was that we couldn't turn around. Where we lived, the highway was only separated by dirt and grass in the middle. So, if you passed up something, all you had to do was make a U-turn across the grass. That wall was preventing us from doing that. In my mind, that meant that we were lost forever going in one direction and not able to turn around. I was terrified and worried for most of the trip.

At one point, I thought that my mother was crying for the same reason because she cried so much. Periodically, Marie would stop at a gas station and ask for directions. To my surprise, we got there eventually, but we were hours behind Rachel by the time we did.

On the way, I remember all of us being amazed at the height of the trees and my mother, who'd drunk spring water my whole life, enjoying the fresh, clean taste of the water fountain at a rest stop in Georgia. I absolutely hated being cramped in that car for hours on end, but it was nice to see my mom smile and look on in awe and amazement instead of crying.

Everything seemed so different than what we were used to. The roads didn't run in a straight line nor were they parallel or perpendicular to each other. Some crossed others slanted; the roads were like rolling hills, one minute you're driving up a hill and the next you're going down.

My one last scare was when we finally turned onto the street where my brother lived. There stood the biggest hill I'd ever seen in my life and we were about to attempt driving over it. Aside from the underpass for the railroad tracks and the levy to the Mississippi River, there were no hills where we had lived. It was all flat land. This was the biggest of all the hills I'd seen so far.

I felt my stomach drop down as if I were on a roller coaster because they took the hill so fast, but in seconds we were over it. I was shocked to see that all the way to the road's end it was downhill. All the townhomes and duplexes, which I'd never heard of or seen before, were unevenly placed all the way down. One person's door would be at one level and the person right next to them would be half a body lower. I'd never seen anything like it, but we'd finally made it to this strange place called Georgia. And, for the first time, my mother kind of seemed like a real live person to me.

CHAPTER 13

THE STRUGGLE TO FIT IN

This place was nothing like where we had come from. Absolutely every aspect of it was different. The scenery, the people, the speech, and most of all, the schools were very different. I remember going to class the first day and immediately not liking it.

See, in my small town you were either black or white, but mostly black. When I went to school there we had mostly black children in the classrooms and maybe a couple of white kids. Here, I was totally out of my comfort zone.

When I walked into the classroom on the first day, there was only one other black kid. On top of that, there weren't just white kids to fill out the rest of the seats. There were races of people that I had never seen before in person. The only other race I had ever encountered as a child was Caucasians.

In this classroom, there were what I later learned: Asians, Hispanics, and Indians who came from India. I learned that the proper word for South Americans was Hispanics because they all came from different countries there and took offense if you called them Mexicans, when they were actually Puerto Rican, Cuban, or Venezuelan, etc. It was the same for the Asians. I had a lot to learn.

I had a stout, white teacher named Mrs. Gray and she had assigned seating, another thing that I disliked. I was upset that she didn't put me at the table with the other black child, Monique. So, I decided to ask her about it and she said if I thought I'd be more comfortable there she'd move me. There was an extra seat open there.

The very next day I got to sit at the table with Monique. I was happy to be there until she spoke to me. I was shocked to hear that she spoke like a white person, as I would have called it at the time. She was very snippy with me because I wasn't following some rule that I didn't even know existed.

It was like that with Monique for the rest of the school year. She was like an enemy to me. I couldn't understand how someone who looked like me could be so different. She didn't like me at all either because I was almost always the cause of our table losing points for the day. She was a stickler for the rules and she disliked me because I didn't follow them.

Mainly it was because I didn't turn in certain homework assignments that were due, but I didn't understand a lot of it. It was third grade and I was ten years old and couldn't grasp things that these kids caught on to very easily. It was as if they had skipped a couple of grades or started off on a higher level. Back at my old school we were still reading picture books. At this school, they were already reading chapter books with no pictures.

They seemed to love these books about Fudge. I hated them because the only pictures were at the beginning of each chapter and it seemed like you had to read forever just to get to the next one. I despised reading these books, they were very boring. My teacher seemed very agitated that I didn't do my work and turn it in when it was due. She also questioned me a lot on whether I was sure I used to make straight A's at my old school. I felt insulted. I was unhappy at this school and I hated the school work.

Once I learned that I wasn't going to get in trouble at home for it, I just stopped doing most of it all together. I only did the work I thought was fun, which was always math. And life became a lot easier for me when the teacher moved me to a different table that didn't care so much about getting points.

Home life wasn't much easier. We lived in a two-bedroom apartment with seven other family members. So, it was my brother Charlie, his girlfriend Celine, her daughter Monet, and their son CJ. There was an older sister, Deidra, from my father's first marriage and her son Gregory and daughter Jaya. Then there was my mother, Daniel, Derrick, me, Matthew, Karen, and Rachel and Reagan who also came to stay later.

My brother, his girlfriend, and their son stayed in one room. All the other females stayed in the other room and all the boys slept downstairs on one sofa bed. I was glad that I didn't have to sleep downstairs because there were roaches everywhere. Some were even crawling over my brothers and nephew when they slept.

My mother didn't like my brother's girlfriend because she wasn't a very clean person. Even though she was home most of the day she didn't really clean anything. So, when we arrived, it was to the dirtiest place I'd ever seen in my life. It seemed like every dish in the kitchen was dirty and the roaches were everywhere. I'd never seen so many roaches and they were all out in broad daylight, all over the dirty dishes, the kitchen counter, the floor and the living room where my brothers and Gregory slept.

My mother was outraged. Charlie and my half-sister, Deidra, worked all day and Deidra also worked at night. She had two or three jobs. No other adults were there during the day except Celine so Mom couldn't understand why she would leave the apartment in such a mess.

Our room was the cleanest and most organized of them all because of my mother. There were beds stretching from one wall to the other and all eight of us slept in one long row. Everything else was packed up against the wall and in the closet.

For some reason, Celine took a liking to me and she asked if I wanted to come and sleep in their room on the twin-size bed with CJ. My brother seemed okay with it so I slept in there one night. At least I tried to go to sleep. Charlie brought back memories of my father because he'd whip my one year old nephew like Dad whipped us. It would break my heart to see him do it because he was only one.

That made for a very uncomfortable night for me. Then when I finally fell asleep I was quickly awakened by noises over on their bed. Charlie was doing a lot of grunting. In the shadows, you could see that he was climbing on top of Celine and he seemed like he was being very rough because their bed was shaking and making a lot of noise. It took me a minute to realize what they were doing.

All I could do is lay there and stare at the scene before me. I could not believe that they would do this right next to me as if I wasn't even there. After the shock wore off I shut my eyes. I didn't want Charlie to catch me staring. I didn't know what he would do if he did, but I didn't want to find out. I laid as still as I possibly could, trying to control my breathing which was becoming labored due to my nervousness. The noises they were making made my stomach turn as if I wanted to throw up.

Then finally they were done and I could hear Charlie slump over to the other side of the bed breathing heavily. I felt like I laid there for hours. The shock of what I had seen and heard making it impossible for my mind to be at ease so that I could fall asleep. I wanted so badly for daylight to come so that I could escape this room and what I had seen.

I must have eventually fallen asleep because when I woke up no one was there. I jumped up and rushed out as fast as I could. The next night they asked if I was coming back and I said no. Charlie just shrugged his shoulders and went on to bed. I don't think it ever dawned on them why I wouldn't go back in there. Most likely, they just didn't care.

I didn't like sleeping in our room either because late at night my nieces, Monet and Jaya, would end up hunching on top of each other right beside me. Then one night Monet was on top of my sister Karen. I didn't say anything, but for some reason I didn't like it. Like Monet was teaching Karen things that I wish she wouldn't learn. Sometimes I wished I didn't know the things that I did. But if Karen wasn't complaining about it I wouldn't get in between them. Maybe she remembered things I had done to her when she was little.

Then one day she saw me watching them and she told Monet to get off. The next day we talked about it. She told me that she didn't like it but Monet kept bothering her to do it. So, that next night I made Karen get behind me up against the wall. Monet went back to hunching Jaya.

Eventually though, it came to my attention that Jaya didn't really like it either. I ended up telling my mother, who in turn told Deidra, Jaya's mom. After that Monet was no longer allowed to sleep in the room with us. She slept in the bed with her baby brother, CJ. Of course, that didn't seem like a better solution to me either. At the time, Monet was probably about seven, Karen was six, and Jaya was five.

Life in that small apartment wasn't fun at all. I'd never seen rooms so small before. I couldn't understand why there was no light fixture in the living rooms of any of these places. I hated the fact that we didn't have our own huge flat yard to play in. Everything was shared.

Even though we grew up with a lot of siblings in the house, there was still room. There were only ever two or three girls to a room. My dad had built a very large, roomy six-bedroom house. I had never felt cramped for space there. Here there was never any privacy, ever. And even though Gregory had a bike we could ride, it was no fun having to strain yourself to ride back up a hill you had so much fun speeding down.

This place was too different and I hated it. If it weren't for my father and all his whippings, I would beg my mother to move back. But there was no going back to that. Even though I'd catch Mom crying at times, she never seemed to long for the life she had. We were stuck here and things didn't look as if they were going to get any better than this.

CHAPTER 14

NEW "PLAYMATES"

When we lived in Louisiana, two men would visit occasionally and speak with my father for a while. I never knew exactly who they were or why they'd come to see him, and strangely, I never asked.

Well, one weekend one of them came over to see Charlie and he spoke kindly to my mother and asked how she was doing. He seemed to really be concerned for her. What surprised me is that this man had driven all those miles to briefly see my brother, or so I thought.

I asked my mother later who he was and she stunned me by saying that he was my brother. "What!" I had said a little too loudly. To this, my older siblings looked at me as if I had grown two heads. I had always known that we had two older sisters from my father's first marriage, but that was it.

That day I learned that my father had a total of six children by his first wife and most of them lived in Georgia, one even living two buildings down from us. So, that day Charlie brought us down to visit the other brother that used to come to visit my father periodically. His wife had the same name as my mother, Mary. They had two sons at the time, one who was my age named after his father, Brice, and a six-year-old named Darrell.

Elroy, who had just visited Charlie, was also over there. He had a girlfriend he'd been with for years named Isabelle. They had two children together, a boy named Roy and a girl whose nickname was Jewel. Elroy also had two older children who lived back in Louisiana. It's funny how I knew that his older two were my niece and nephew, but didn't realize that he was their father or my brother for that matter.

I guess I didn't know who they were because they all lived in Georgia and when they came to visit, no one had ever announced how they were related to us. My father had two boys and four girls from his first marriage. So, all in all, he had sixteen children and his first wife also had one more child that we called our step sister.

My father's oldest and youngest daughters from his first marriage didn't really socialize with us, but when we'd have family gatherings the other four siblings would usually show up. They'd also invite us to whatever they had going on. That's when we'd usually see the other two, but they'd only be polite and speak.

Brice's sons had lots of toys and treats so I'd always end up down the street playing with them. It was much nicer there and Mary kept her house very clean. I remember she'd always wipe everything down with bleach, especially after she had company.

I didn't much like playing with my nephew Brice. Even though we were the same age, he was huge. Brice was always very strong and heavy set and he played with a heavy hand. He'd do things that would purposely hurt me, like karate chop me in the throat, and then he'd laugh about it. I never knew where he got his size from because his father was built like my father, muscular yet slim at the same time.

I'd always end up playing with Darrell and he'd go off to play basketball or something with my brothers. I stopped playing with my brothers because of Brice. Darrell was very nice though. He'd let me play with all his trucks, cars, Legos, and action figures. He had everything and we'd sit and play together for hours.

Sometimes we'd wrestle and one day while we were wrestling he ended up on my back. I fell to the floor pretending that he was too heavy. That's when I felt something hard up against my bottom. When I stopped moving he hunched up against my butt a few times, then he waited.

I was shocked that he knew about this so I turned over and asked, "Do you want to play like that?" He looked at me seriously and said yes. That day we ended up hunching until I climaxed. When I got up I asked him not to tell his mother and he said he never does. Obviously, he had been doing things like this with someone else.

Sometimes my older siblings would all drop their kids off to Mom and go play pool or go out together. By this time, it was summer and my mother had moved into the apartment complex just behind the elementary school. They'd all come and drop their children off until late that night or the next day. Mom would watch us all. Most times she'd just stay in her room though because we were all old enough to take care of the younger kids.

Everyone else was in the back of our 3-bedroom apartment playing video games and things. Darrell and Roy were up front in the living room with me. Darrell said that he wanted us all to wrestle so we did. Roy was about eight or nine at the time and I was almost eleven. When Darrell said how he wanted to play he looked at Roy in a funny way and smiled.

I found out why after a few minutes of playing because both Roy and Darrell ended up taking turns hunching with me. I played like that with them until I climaxed and then we stopped. Afterwards we went back to playing like normal.

Every time they came over we'd always end up hunching at some point. If there were too many people around inside the apartment and it was daylight, we'd go outside and hunch in the woods. Sometimes when they slept over we would stay up until everyone went to bed and do it.

We'd get free cable for a week from the cable company periodically, as a promotion to get my mom to order cable. She never did, but when we had cable there were these channels where grown-ups had sex all day. Even though the picture was blurred you could still make out what they were doing if you stared long enough and the sound wasn't cut off so you could hear it.

Sometimes just Roy and his sister would come over and

we used to watch it late at night and Roy would always take out his penis and play with it while I watched. This was when we started hunching with our pants and underwear pulled down. Eventually, I started doing the same thing with Darrell and Daniel.

Everything that I did with Darrell and Roy was always separate from what I did with Daniel. I thought that if Daniel knew that I was doing these things he would tell my mother. Plus, it was different with Darrell and Roy. Whenever I was finished we would stop. With Daniel, if I finished before him I would have to lie underneath him and just wait until he finished. Once I was done I never wanted to lay there and wait.

Plus, different things started to happen with Daniel. Some things happened that I liked and some that I didn't. Daniel taught me how to stroke his penis. I liked that because I liked looking at it while I did it. What I didn't like was when he would beg to kiss me and I hated when he'd try to put his tongue in my mouth. It was the nastiest thing ever.

Then when we'd hunch with our pants down his body would start shaking right before he finished and this stuff would come out of his penis. I didn't like that at all, especially if I was already done. I didn't pay much attention to it if I wasn't done yet, but if I was I'd always feel so disgusted afterwards. Either way, I'd go to the bathroom immediately after that and clean it off.

This was when things started not to be so pleasurable

with Daniel. He had just turned fourteen. I felt like he was changing and he wanted different things than I did. He'd always ask questions about doing something different when all I wanted to do was hunch and get it over with.

I didn't want to stop doing things with him altogether because I did like some of the changes. One was that his penis seemed very large and I could feel it more when we hunched. While he wanted to do more things, different things, I just wanted what we did to stay the same.

No kissing, no putting his tongue in my mouth, and definitely no slimy white substance coming from his penis. These were things I just could not and did not want to get used to. But I still liked hunching him, mainly because of the size of his penis. So, I just continued to adamantly say no to the kissing and put up with having to clean myself off afterwards.

CHAPTER 15

MARIE BRINGS SUNSHINE

When summer started my sister Marie and her husband Frank moved up to Georgia. They rented a town home at the top of the hill just before my mom got her apartment on the next street over.

I was so happy to see Marie because she always introduced us to new things. She was the one who had started Christmas in our home. When she had gotten married and moved across town in Louisiana, she would always come and get us and we'd do something fun. She was the one to acquaint us with movie rentals, something I'd never known existed.

When she moved to Georgia it was the same. Marie was very exploratory. She researched what was considered fun in Georgia and that summer we did a lot. I think the one thing that was the most fun was riding the MARTA train to go and see Underground Atlanta. I wasn't very impressed by the Underground, but I loved riding the train.

When she started school in Atlanta she would often

take Matthew and I with her. We'd ride the train and walk to her classes, then sit outside the room and wait until her class was done. I didn't even mind the waiting because I lived for the train rides and she would always buy us fast food.

There were so many different fast food places to choose from, it was crazy! Down in Louisiana I had only ever heard of McDonald's, Burger King, Popeye's, Pizza Hut, and Dairy Queen. Our small town sported Pizza Hut, Popeye's, Dairy Queen, and a very recently built McDonald's before we moved. We had taken a field trip there to get some ice cream; it was a big deal. Burger King I knew of from commercials.

It was the same with the retail and grocery stores. We only had a Winn Dixie and Wal-Mart. Besides hearing about Piggly Wiggly on commercials, I had no idea that there were more fast food and retail chains. Publix, Kroger, and Ingles were all foreign to me; as well as Checkers, Arby's, Wendy's, etc. I could go on forever about things I'd never seen or heard of, including shopping malls. These things were new to me and some, a bit shocking.

During that summer, she also took us to see Stone Mountain along with our older half-brothers and their families. I began to have an appreciation for Georgia that I did not have when I first arrived. There were a lot of beautiful things to see and do. It may not be a big deal to some, but I think what I appreciated the most was the cleanliness.

Where I lived in Louisiana I don't think there were any littering laws. Riding down the road people threw trash out of the windows all the time. When other kids walked through our yard they would discard trash on the grass and just keep going. We were constantly sent outside by our father to pick up trash out of the yard.

In Georgia, you weren't allowed to do these things. You would get a ticket for throwing trash from a car window. The streets where we lived were very beautiful. For miles and miles, I would ride in the car and just stare out the window at perfectly cut grass, bushes, and trees. I especially liked all the colorful flowers that were growing around the bushes and trees. Marie took us to see a lot that summer and by summer's end I was in love with Georgia.

Marie knew that we hadn't been happy in Georgia. I think she had a talk with Mom and she had been expressing how hard it was to be here, especially when we weren't happy here either. I was glad that I no longer got whippings, but before Marie came, life in Georgia was very depressing. She had sat us all down and told us that we had to be on our best behavior and make the most of this new place. She had said that the two of us that did our best were going to be able to go with her and Frank the next time they visited Louisiana.

By the end of that summer Marie kept her promise and picked Matthew and I to travel with them to Louisiana the next time they visited. We were so excited to go. The trip went very well; the only boring part was visiting relatives. We also spent time at Frank's parent's house. That was fun because his mother was very nice and every single day she cooked some good Cajun food.

Frank's nephew Roderick also stayed with Frank's mother so we had someone to play with. When it was time to leave that night, he begged Marie to take him with her to sleep over where we were at Frank's sister's house. She let him come with us. Matthew and I stayed up late playing video games with him.

When everyone in the house, including Matthew, was asleep he turned off the lights and came to sit close to me. Roderick put his hand on my upper thigh and put his fingers to his lips to signal for me to be quiet and I nodded my head in understanding. Then he took my hand and started rubbing it against his crotch area.

Matthew was across the room snoring so I knew for sure that he was asleep. In the dark Roderick let me push him down to the floor, climb on top of him, and hunch him. When I was finished, I got off and sat beside him. He didn't say a word, he just sat there and smiled at me for a moment then he went over to where his covers were and we both lay down to go to sleep. Two or three times he lifted his head to smile at me and I'd smile back.

All I kept thinking was that this was the best time I'd ever had here. I had just turned eleven and I think Roderick was still ten. But, most importantly, I liked it with him the best because he wasn't my relative. So, I mostly didn't feel bad about what I had done with him. The only thing that bothered me was that Marie brought me here for good behavior. She thought I was good. Had she known what I'd done, I think she would've been very disappointed.

CHAPTER 16

GETTING INTO THE SWING OF THINGS

Fourth grade wasn't as hard as third. This time around I had a male teacher. That was a first for me. The only part of fourth grade that was challenging at first was the periodicals we had to write. Every week we had to find an article in the newspaper to read and then write about what we had read.

I got off to a rocky start because I seemed to be the only kid in class that didn't have access to the newspaper and had no idea how to write a summary or what the word summary even meant.

After a couple of weeks of not turning in the assignment Mr. Elam had a talk with me about it. I told him why I was having such a hard time. He then told the class that he would bring in a few newspapers every Monday and that we would have the rest of the week to turn in our assignment.

After explaining the assignment in detail, he also told me that if I had any other problems, I could talk to him about them and he would see what we could do. He was different from Mrs. Gray and I liked that he didn't come at me with an accusatory tone when he spoke to me. Mr. Elam always had a "let's see what we can do about this" approach to any learning issue I had. That year school became easy again.

By the end of it, Mr. Elam was the best teacher I'd ever had and he even kept some of my artwork for years after I left there. He always thought that I was very smart and artistic. It excited me that I would do certain things in art class and he would ask me if he could keep some of them. The next day I'd see something I sculpted on his desk holding his pens and pencils or a drawing up on the wall.

My mom never cared about these things. I'd take them home to show her and all she would say is, "Uh huh." Sometimes I felt like she hadn't even taken a good look at it because, for some reason, when I showed them to Mr. Elam or the art teacher they were always so enthusiastic about what I made. Between the two of them I didn't bring a lot of things home.

I also got a taste of chorus in the fourth grade. After the first nine weeks, Mrs. Harrison encouraged me to try out for chorus and I did. So, I had chorus after school two or three times a week. Sometimes I would ask to stay after school on the days that we didn't have chorus because I never really wanted to go home. After that she became my mentor, but they called it something else that I can't remember. I didn't fully understand back then, but for some reason she picked me.

Our chorus got to go to all different types of places

to sing. The field trips did cost money but one of the teachers always ended up paying for me to go because Mom didn't have the money. Even if we did a concert at school and it was free, Mom still did not attend. She was always afraid that someone would try to make her read something even though I'd tell her otherwise.

I don't know why I'd always think, maybe this time she'll come. It never happened and I began to get angry because of it. I just didn't understand what was so hard about coming to sit and watch me sing.

One day, when I stayed after school with Mrs. Harrison, she started teaching me how to play the piano. I was very excited about this. She would try to get me to sing for her also, but I didn't think I could sing all that well so I never did. It was easier singing with a group than having all the attention focused on you. I was not confident in my abilities, and very scared to sing alone.

During our after-school time together she would always ask me about my mother and my home life. She never made any comments about what I'd tell her, but she always looked sad when we'd have these talks. I was always careful never to tell her anything that would get me into trouble though. She would never know what I did with certain relatives when alone with them.

All three of these teachers gave me a love for school that I hadn't really had before. School was like an escape to another world. A world that was fair. A place where all you had to do was try your best and you'd do great.

I was not the only child making good grades that year. Karen had also made the honor roll a few times. But where I would keep my awards tucked away in a safe place she would have them strewn all over our room just like the rest of her stuff. I thought that awards were so important and she didn't seem to care for them.

I decided for myself that I would keep them for her. I thought that maybe she would come to cherish them as I had always done with mine. When that day came, my plan had been to give them back to her. It didn't work out that way though. Over the two years that I was in elementary school I had picked up three or four of her honor roll ribbons. When I had put them away with mine I hadn't separated them.

So, by the time she did notice that they were missing they had already become a part of my collection. When she asked me what I had done with them, that she wanted them back, I gave her a snide remark that she should never have left them hanging about in the first place. I told her that that's what she got for leaving them out.

As she looked at me angrily and with resentment, I knew that I was wrong. But I just couldn't part with them. Some of her ribbons were so fresh and new where the bold print on mine had been worn from me always touching and handling them. From then on it seemed that she never looked at me the same again, but I just put it all out of my mind. I just couldn't give them back to her. No matter the consequence, in my eyes they were mine now.

CHAPTER 17

CHARLIE IN CHAINS

Charlie and Mom took a trip to Louisiana during my fourth-grade school year. Mom left a pregnant Samantha in charge of me, Daniel, Derrick, Matthew, and Karen. I hated it because she would make us little kid sized meals and when we'd complain that we were still hungry she wouldn't care. We were just told we'd have to wait until the next meal and she'd do the same thing all over again.

On their way down to Louisiana, Charlie was doing his normal, speeding. Charlie almost always drove more than the speed limit. What made it worse is when he would get angry. You never knew what he was capable of when he was angry. Sometimes he'd be doing 85mph, in 45 mph traffic, with a good bit of cars on the road.

That was the scariest time because he'd appear to be about to ram someone in the rear, but at the last minute he'd duck around them only to get behind another car. He'd whip in and out of traffic as if he were playing a video game, like our lives didn't matter. If he couldn't get around a car he would drive on the shoulder. Once, he got so aggravated with the stand still traffic that he went over the cement median in the middle of the road just to go the other way.

When he was on the interstate it was less scary even though he would drive faster. Where cars couldn't move out of his way on regular roads they saw him coming on the interstate. Usually they would move before he got near enough to them for it to be scary. The entire time he was driving, someone in the car would be pleading for him to slow down, but he'd keep speeding as if no one was even there speaking to him. Sometimes it would make him even angrier and he'd drive faster.

Sometime after they'd left for Louisiana Mom called and said that Charlie had been arrested. She'd said that he'd driven like a bat out of hell up until they pulled him over. He had been driving so fast that the cops came at him cautiously with hands on their guns yelling at him to step out of the car. Mom was afraid for his life so she also got out of the passenger side to make sure that they wouldn't shoot him.

That's when they pulled out their guns, prepared to shoot. Charlie yelled for them not to shoot Mom because their guns were aimed at her. She had gotten out of the car without their permission. I think on top of him driving like a maniac he also had a warrant out for his arrest because of previous speeding tickets that he had not paid.

So, Mom had called to say that Charlie had been arrested and she was stuck at the police department. No one from our home town in Louisiana could come and get her, it was too far. Mom would never go anywhere by herself because she didn't know how to read. She was stranded there.

The next morning before school, she called to say that she was still there. That day I went to school sad. I had chorus with Mrs. Harrison and she pulled me aside to ask what was wrong. After I told her she seemed very concerned, but she told me that she was sure everything would be fine. Later that day, before school let out, she came to my class and asked to speak with me. She gave me her home phone number and told me that she could go and get my mom if she was still stranded at that police station. I was to go home and get my sister to call her if Mom still needed a ride home.

I went home happy, knowing that Mom had a way back home. I had been worried that she would be stuck there forever if Charlie didn't get out of jail. I came home excitedly telling Sam the good news. Immediately she got angry and couldn't believe that I had told our personal business to a teacher.

I found out then that they had let Charlie go and they were already on their way back home. Sam told me that she was going to tell Mom as soon as she got home and that I was going to be in big trouble. So, as usual, I had to wait it out in fear. I didn't know what Mom would do, but I was more afraid of Charlie because he gave whippings like my father did.

When Mom got home, one of the first things Sam blurted out was what I had done, as if she could not wait until Mom got in the door. I felt like she had been anticipating my punishment. Mom just looked at me and said, "Oh, really?" I didn't get a punishment that day. She was only surprised that a teacher would reach out and do something so grand. She even told me to extend her thanks to the teacher for her generous offer of help.

Charlie had not come into the house when he dropped Mom off. I was so thankful for that because he had been very angry at the turn of events and there's no telling what he would have been capable of. I went back to school the next day relieved and happy that I had such good news to convey.

CHAPTER 18

COMING HOME FAT

Mom sent us to our dad for the summer. All of us except Matthew went. He was the first to think to ask if he could stay and she let him because he was just one compared to the five she usually had. Six, if you counted Sam who had already left to go back to Louisiana. She had a boyfriend that had gotten her pregnant so she went to be close to him, but she stayed with Dad.

Mom also had a soft spot for Matthew; I think it was because he was her youngest boy. That's also why I think she let him stay. I knew she'd needed a break and some time to save up money for the next school year so I went along with no fuss.

Dad had seemed different to me when we visited with Frank and Marie. When other siblings went to visit, he would have a hard time with who was who and he never got our ages right. They'd always laugh about it because he couldn't remember. He'd even ask us how we were doing. All of that made me more comfortable with going to visit with him for a summer. He seemed different in a good way.

That all changed when Mom dropped us off and

went back home. He changed in a heartbeat, almost as soon as she was far enough away not to come back and get us. As long as she was there for the weekend I went outside and came back as I pleased. The very next day I woke up and dressed to go outside and he asked where we thought we were going, Karen and I.

When I told him we were going outside he told us no and to sit back down, that we weren't going anywhere. He said that we were nothing but a bunch of whores and all we would do is go outside and get pregnant. I was almost twelve that summer and Karen was only seven.

I was appalled. Not only did my father call us whores, but he also stated that we, being eleven and seven years of age, would go out and get pregnant. It wasn't a question in his mind, it was a fact. He had said this with such conviction and vehemence that I was taken aback, shocked into silence.

I didn't know what to say or do for fear of his next move. Not only that, but Sam was sitting right there and had not said a word or even looked offended by it for our sakes. He then walked away and left all three of us girls in the living room while Daniel and Derrick ran out the door to go play.

I asked Sam if she had heard what Dad said and she said she had and then proceeded to ask me what she was supposed to do about it. I was outraged; she just sat there and went back to watching the television as if nothing happened. For the entire summer, it went on that way. My father was the oppressor and Sam was the enforcer.

Karen and I couldn't go anywhere unless Sam or my

father was going. Sam didn't want to go anywhere because it was extremely hot and she was pregnant. The only place that my father ever took us was to the grocery store where he bought us whatever we wanted to eat.

In my case, it was junk food, boxed macaroni and cheese, and tater tots. Basically, all I ate were fattening foods. I was not happy. I couldn't believe that Sam would enforce my father's craziness on us when he wasn't there, but she did as he said. She never let us go outside.

By the time Marie came to get us at the end of the summer all she could complain about is how fat Karen and I had gotten. She couldn't understand how we could gain so much weight in one summer, just the two of us. But she asked all this in front of my father and, of course, I had no words for it.

I had gained twenty pounds that summer. All I had done for two months is sit in front of the TV and eat. Though I had wanted to go outside every single day of those two months, I was not allowed. I felt like I was six years old all over again. It was the worst summer ever.

The only good thing about it is that Sam's boyfriend had come by on my birthday and given me twenty dollars. It was the most money anyone had ever given to me at one time. But during the trip home my mother hadn't given Marie enough money to make it back so she used my money for gas.

When she saw that I was upset about it she reassured me that Mom would give my money back because she would make sure she told her she had taken it from me. I was still sad, remembering the time I had saved for a bike. I knew better than to believe it, but I was stupid enough just to hold out a little hope.

She kept her promise to me when we got home and she did tell our mother that it was my birthday money. But, just as I feared, I never saw that money again. Even though Mom had told Marie she would give it back. The few times that I did approach her about it she said that all I would do was buy junk food with it and I was already fat enough.

Mom was very upset about us coming home fat. I told her what Dad had done. She was upset that he had done it, but she was also upset with me too. She said I had had a choice and I knew better than to eat like I had. On my end, I felt like if I couldn't have fun any other way; I would at least enjoy eating.

I grew a little more depressed after that summer because Daniel, Derrick, and Matthew started to tease me even more because I had gotten fatter. I started to feel like I couldn't do anything right.

CHAPTER 19

FRIENDS

In fourth grade, I came to the realization that I was taller than everyone else, all except one other black girl. In fifth grade, I was glad to see that I ended up in the same classroom with her. Skye was her name and, since my last name was right after hers alphabetically, we stood in line together every day, which made me very happy.

Fifth grade was a very awkward year for me. I was twelve years old and I no longer felt comfortable in my own body. I wore a jacket to school every single day under the pretense that it was cold in the classroom. Having Skye there made me feel somewhat normal even though, like everyone else, she was ten years old.

That year there were quite a few black kids in class. There was one other girl that I hadn't seen at school last year and she seemed very quiet. I had become very talkative by then, so I made it a point to speak to her because she was new and didn't seem to have any friends. Skye and I approached her at recess. Her name was Laila and from then on out we were the three musketeers.

They were my first real friends since I'd moved to

Georgia. When my mom had gotten her own apartment there were lots of other kids in the complex, but I was so used to being inside by then that I would never feel like going outside. They would even come to the door and ask for me and beg me to come outside, most times I didn't though.

In Louisiana, we almost never had friends over because my parents didn't allow it. No one ever wanted to come inside of our house anyway because of our father. I, personally, had never had a friend over, it was out of the question as far as I was concerned.

But these friends at school, I liked them and I had a different relationship with each one. With Skye, we'd always joke back and forth and tease and laugh most of the time. When we were with Laila at recess we did much of the same, but Laila would mostly just laugh, she wouldn't say much. We'd even tease Laila sometimes because she was so quiet, but all she would do is smile and giggle.

The only times that Laila would speak was when they brought up the fact that I spoke differently. They'd tease me about it sometimes and try to get me to repeat what I said when it sounded funny. Instead of saying "for real?" when asking if something really happened I'd say, "for true?" Instead of backpack or book bag, it was book sack. Behind almost every sentence I would say yea or no. There were a lot of things I said or pronounced differently. There was obviously a huge difference between having a southern accent and an accent from Louisiana. But it was all in fun.

I'd always wish that I could spend more time with

Laila, but I couldn't because everything happened in alphabetical order. I think Skye felt the same way because whenever we would have to line up after being together, she would wave goodbye to Laila with this dramatically sad face and I would follow suit. Then when Laila would do the same we'd all end up giggling. With them there was always laughter.

If I ever got to spend time with just Laila, I wasn't as loud as I was when Skye was around. Skye brought out my natural loud, fun side. With Laila, I always ended up having more serious conversations because my aim was always to get her to talk. I think I was more attached to Laila because she was always so quiet and accepting of me where sometimes Skye would talk over me and be very opinionated and against some of the things I would do or want to do.

CHAPTER 20

SIMEON

Samantha went into labor in the middle of the night and had Simeon on Halloween. My mom had gotten Karen and I up out of our sleep and took us with them to the hospital. She left the boys at the apartment by themselves. I was very excited about my sister having a baby. This was my first time being at a hospital when someone was having one.

I remember being sent back and forth to get ice for Samantha because she couldn't eat any food. For hours, she just chewed and chewed on ice. I had been under the impression that when your water broke you immediately went to the doctor and had the baby. I was wrong.

We stayed there for what I remember to be about eighteen hours waiting for Samantha to become fully dilated. It was taking forever and boredom quickly set in. Occasionally, Karen and I had to stand outside of the room while Samantha was being examined to see if she had dilated enough. I was amazed that the doctor wasn't even there.

When she did get there, she asked Samantha if she wanted us all to stay in the room while she had her baby. A discussion ensued about Karen and I being old enough to stay.

I got excited then. I wanted to stay. I kept begging Samantha to let me stay. All she kept saying was that she would think about it. So, finally I just got quiet and thought that maybe if I didn't say anything when the time came she would forget that we were there.

When her time did come, she allowed us to stay and during most of it I was wishing that she hadn't. They sat us both on her right side at the head of the bed. Mom was standing a little farther down where she could see the baby coming out. I was afraid because we were right by her head and she kept throwing up yellow liquid.

On top of that she was screaming in pain and her lips were white and chapped looking. It seemed like chaos everywhere though I'm certain now that the doctor had everything under control. I kept thinking to myself that if having a baby was so painful and messy, why did women keep having them and talking like it's the greatest thing?

When the baby finally came out he had slimy, brown looking stuff all over him and it looked gross to me. A nurse took him to the other side of the room and started cleaning him off. She called me over and asked if I wanted to see. I hopped up quickly because anything was better than the imminent threat of yellow vomit.

By the time I came over he was all cleaned up and screaming at the top of his lungs. He was a big baby, nine pounds and seven ounces with a head full of hair. They said that Samantha needed stitches because he'd torn her coming out. He had a cone head because they'd used a suction cup to help pull him out.

The nurse asked me if I would wash my hands and hold his feet because she needed to take blood in a minute but his feet were too cold. When I grabbed a hold of them he calmed down and stopped crying. I was surprised and honored at the same time. All I could do was stand there and smile. I felt sorry for him when she did stick him though.

I wrote about the experience for computer class and it was made into a book by Mr. Elam. I was so happy about it. When I came home and showed it to Samantha she took it and kept it. That's the first thing I ever remember a family member taking and cherishing. As for my opinion of the entire experience, I vowed to never have sex or get pregnant.

CHAPTER 21

MISBEHAVING

Fifth grade also marked a turning point in my behavior at school. When I was at home Mom never really engaged us in any kind of conversation or activities. By this time, she had gotten a job working and was getting paid minimum wage, which in turn cut off the welfare and most of the food stamps.

Back then I think minimum wage was $4.75 an hour. As soon as my mother got that job working full time the state agency would cut the assistance off. I just couldn't understand why that would happen. Those were scary times. Mom never made enough to pay all the bills even when she was on welfare and I thought for sure that these people knew this. So, why would they take most of the help she was getting away, just because she got a job that didn't bring in much more than that? It made no sense to me.

We ate better when my mother didn't have a job. So, when she did have a job that made school essential because, at least we got something good for breakfast and lunch. Other kids thought school food was gross, but I thought it was great! Most times we did have something to eat at home, but it wasn't a real meal. We'd eat mayonnaise sandwiches or rice and butter because they were the cheapest things that she could buy a lot of. Mostly it was rice though, because she could buy a fifty-pound bag for a low price.

Mom also put a lot of responsibility on me when she was working, that never made sense to me either because I wasn't the oldest, Daniel and Derrick were. At the time, Samantha would come and stay for a few months and then she would move back to Louisiana. Reagan didn't like it here because she was in high school and at the top of her class in Louisiana. She didn't like the school here and she missed her friends so she begged mom to let her move back and she did.

I was the oldest girl in the house so Mom expected me to keep the apartment clean. She would come home every day and fuss at me for not having things just the way she would have had them. Even if I tried my best, she would always find something wrong with the way I did it. I could never live up to her standards and every day I'd just get angrier.

What made it worse is that my brothers didn't try to help. They'd come home from school or get up on the weekends and it was like a tornado crashed through the kitchen. They would cook things and leave dirty pots and dishes everywhere. And when Mom came home she would never ask who did these things, she would always ask why I hadn't cleaned it up. This was the type of attention I got from her daily.

I think Mom upheld certain ideals from the way my dad raised us. The boys' only chores were to take out the trash and cut the grass and that's if my dad didn't tell one of the girls to do it. The girls did everything else. I remember being nine or ten and it taking me two hours to clean the kitchen after dinner. Including my father's mother, thirteen people had eaten at every meal in our house. The only difference now was that the apartment complex cut the grass so my brothers had even less to do than before.

I was still in chorus, Skye was there also, but I was no longer allowed to stay after with Mrs. Harrison. She couldn't be my mentor two years in a row, that wouldn't be fair to another student. I didn't see Mr. Elam much because he had become the computer teacher and his computer room was on a different hallway than the fifth graders. I didn't get much attention from grown-ups at all.

In my neighborhood, I was considered someone other kids my age shouldn't mess with because I'd beat up kids sometimes. It was only because I caught them picking on other kids so; I thought they should see how it feels to either get beat up by someone bigger or fight someone their own size. Either way, I'd beat them up and I justified it because they shouldn't have been picking on someone else.

At school, I'd always get in trouble with the teacher because I was talking or laughing during class. One day she decided to take me out into the hallway to talk to me. When she did, she got close to me and put her finger in my face. That made me angry and in return I used some pretty profane language and told her that her breath stinks. I thought she would send me to the principal's office, but that wasn't the reaction I got.

Instead, she broke down and started crying in front of me. I was shocked, but I didn't feel sorry at all. I felt powerful. I was bad enough to make a teacher cry, that made me feel good. Like, for once, I was in control. I left her out there in the hallway crying. I went and sat back down in my seat, folded my arms, and smiled thinking that I sure showed her.

Everyone was looking at me in amazement because they couldn't believe what they were hearing and seeing. No one had ever done anything like that to a teacher. And somehow, I felt like I had reached some new status among the students. And even though it was bad, it felt good.

After that I continued to talk to her in the same way whenever she would try to bring me in hand. Sometimes I'd get brave enough to do it during class and in front of everyone. When that happened she'd always leave the room for a few minutes. While she was gone, the students used to make comments about how bad I was, but I liked it. When she would return, her eyes would be slightly red and puffy and I'd be satisfied with what I had accomplished.

Then one day rumors surfaced that a white girl in my neighborhood named Kristy was going around school calling me a bitch. I didn't even know this girl that well and I couldn't believe she had the audacity to call me a name. This was something that I had to deal with.

If I let her go around school calling me names and I didn't do anything about it, then everyone else would think they could. Truth be told, every time I fought someone I was scared and nervous about losing, even though I never did. I didn't really want to fight this girl, but to keep up with my reputation I had to. Everyone kept asking me what I was going to do about it and I told them all that I was going to beat her up at recess.

What made it even better was that Laila and Skye said they were going to help me jump her because she had been picking at them also. The problem with that was, when we went to approach the girl, they were talking about a different Kristy. This girl was black. I promised them that I would have their backs so I stayed with them when they approached her.

Of course, when she saw us she ended up apologizing to them because she was afraid to fight. Once that was done, I sought out the Kristy I was looking for. She was all the way on the other side of the playground. As I was walking over to confront her, my heart beat faster with every step. The crowd behind me also grew bigger as I progressed.

By the time I reached her I had at least thirty other students behind me. I called her name and she turned to face me. As soon as I had her attention I said, "I heard that you've been going around school calling me a-" I didn't even get the word out, she had already reared back and punched me in the face.

Luckily, it didn't hurt at all and immediately my reflexes kicked in. I took her by the front of her dress with both hands and slammed her to the ground. Within seconds most of the school yard was surrounding us and chanting the word fight. They expected me to do more; I could see it in their eyes. So, I lifted my right foot and began kicking her repeatedly.

She tried to stop me by grabbing my leg and attempting to bite me. I switched to my left foot and kicked her in the face. Her glasses fell off. The buttons running down the front of her dress started popping off and coming a loose with every subsequent kick.

By this point I was unreasonably angry. I was angry because she had gotten in the first lick. I was angry at the entire situation. Most of all, I was just plain angry and a good bit of it had nothing to do with her.

I remember someone much bigger than me pulling me off her, but I didn't get a chance to turn and see who it was because right then the principal came into my line of vision. Boy, did he look angry. "In my office, now!" he yelled to me with his finger pointed in that direction.

"Oooooh!" was all I heard from the other students as I walked away. I was in big trouble now. I turned to take one last look and saw a teacher and the principal helping Kristy, who was crying hysterically, up off the ground.

It took Mr. Parker a while to get back to his office, so I had a lot of time to sit and think. I had about a three inch burn on my upper arm where my youngest sister, Karen, had accidently knocked the iron over on it a week or so before. I had been lying down on the floor ironing my chorus shirt as she sat beside me.

I was now sitting in a chair in front of his desk angrily picking at the huge scab the burn had left behind. I remember the skin I uncovered looking very pink, almost reddish in color. I had decided that I didn't care what he came in here and said or did to me; I was not going to cry like I had in kindergarten.

When he came in and sat down the first thing he said was, "What happened?" It never occurred to me that he wouldn't automatically blame it on me. That disarmed me and I told him verbatim what had transpired. Surprisingly, he said that my story lined up with the other students, unlike hers. He had asked questions and actually listened for the answers?

This was all new to me. Most of the time my father would ask a question, but before you could open your mouth to answer he would already be in mid swing. This man was also different from the last principal I'd encountered. I found myself starting to like him until he said that I would have to pay for her glasses because I'd broken them.

Immediately, I got angry and told him that I, neither my mother was paying for anything because she started that fight and all I did was finish it. He proceeded to try and explain to me why I was indeed going to pay for them. All I did was sit there and start angrily picking at my scab again.

Suddenly, he stopped talking in mid-sentence and asked, "What happened to you!" It didn't come out as a question, more like an angry demand. At that I looked up in alarm, but then I calmed down when I realized he was talking about my arm. I explained to him what happened and he looked at me as if I had told him a lie.

He left the room and came back in with the school nurse who seemed as shaken as he was at the sight of it. She proceeded to tell him that there was nothing she needed to do to it now because it was obviously healing if there was a scab. Then she told me that I should stop picking at it, but I didn't listen. After that the principal took her outside the room to speak with her once more.

When he came back he asked me if I was sure that the burn was an accident. I looked at him stupidly for a moment and then snapped that yes, I was sure. He sat for a minute thinking. I guess he decided to let that issue drop because his next words were that he was going to have to suspend me from school for a week.

At the time, we didn't have a phone so he couldn't contact my mother, but he did send me home with the paperwork for her to sign. My suspension started the day after I brought the papers back. I enjoyed being home alone for a week. The only downside was that I missed out on all the school food.

Mom never punished me for it, she just signed the papers. When I got back to school I was looked at almost in awe by the other students and I loved every minute of it. So much so that I did anything I could to make it to the principal's office, including getting angry enough to walk out of the classroom and all the way home.

I knew Mom was off from work that day and that she

would let me in. She didn't fuss. She just asked me why I was there and when I told her that the teacher made me angry so I left, she just accepted it and continued to watch television.

The next thing I knew, there was a knock at the door. I got up to answer and was shocked down to my toes to see the principal standing there asking for my mother. He and my mom talked for a few minutes about my behavior while I just stood there, arms crossed and angrily staring at him. She promised him that we were going to have a talk when he left. I knew exactly what that meant.

She wasn't going to do anything. My mom's talks consisted of one sentence, "You better not do that again." "That" encompassed everything that any school official would ever discuss with her. All I would ever say was okay and then I'd be back to my usual like she hadn't said a thing.

CHAPTER 22

SELF-CONSCIOUS ME

Things started to change in fifth grade. I was twelve years old and I had started growing breasts. It was very uncomfortable because at recess the boys would run around and snap the bras of girls who had breasts. I never wanted anyone to notice that I had them.

My sisters noticed and it was a constant subject to tease me about. My brothers were always teasing me, calling me fat and ugly all the time, especially Daniel. I was glad that he never asked to see them because he'd treat me like I was disgusting when around Derrick and Matthew.

My mother kept trying to dress me in feminine clothes that clung to my body in ways I didn't like. That made everything ten times worse. My solution to all of this was to wear a jacket to school every single day, no matter the weather. Laila and Skye would try their best to coerce me to take it off, it never worked. It could be the hottest day ever recorded and I'd still have that jacket on.

Someone had given my mother a bag of hand me down clothing one day. That happened a lot being that she couldn't afford new clothes for us most of the time. I was the first to sift through it and I had found a green Florida Gators button down baseball shirt with orange pinstripes in it. I had also gotten a pair of orange jean shorts from a next-door neighbor that matched perfectly with that shirt.

Both items were considered boy's clothing, but I loved that outfit. That was the only outfit that I would wear to school without a jacket. I couldn't wait to wear it. Every day after wearing it I was sad because I had to take it off and put it in the wash. It was the most comfortable thing I felt that I had ever worn on my body. I would usually wear that outfit twice a week if I could, once at school and once on the weekend.

The neighbor that had given me the shorts would always shake her head when she'd see me with that outfit on because I'd wear it so much. Thus, began my fascination with men's clothing. Women's clothing was meant to enhance certain features. I wanted to hide them and that's what the men's clothing provided.

Towards the end of the fifth-grade school year most everything was still the same. I was still fighting in and out of school, terrorizing my teacher, and wearing a jacket to school every day. By now Skye and I were good friends and I considered Laila to be my best friend. Having good friends was a great feeling for me. I started to feel like I was wanted.

I got to visit with my 4th grade teacher, Mr. Elam, sometimes. This was the school year that I was introduced to poetry and we could type up short stories and poems on the computer. Mr. Elam made them out of real books. He seemed to take an interest in my poetry after he'd made books of our poetry projects. He thought that mine were very good and encouraged me to keep writing.

The only thing I was really worried about at this point was the upcoming parent/student picnic the school had for the fifth graders at the end of the year. In the two years that I'd been at the school my mother had come to only one thing. That was one of our chorus performances and it was only because Marie came with her. I didn't hold out hope anymore. I knew that she would never attend anything I had at school alone.

It's just that all the fifth graders were going to eat on the school lawn that day, whether their parents came or not. I didn't want to be the only one sitting out there without a parent for all to see. I was terrified of what everyone would think of me. I would be so uncomfortable sitting out there feeling like everyone was looking at me, talking about me.

I had asked Laila and Skye if their parents were coming and they'd both said yes. That was the clincher for me. Had at least one of them said no, I wouldn't have felt so inferior. Then I would've been happy because I would have someone else to sit with, someone I liked, a friend.

I had decided that I wasn't going to go to school that day. It was either that or walk home for lunch, in which case I may have been dragged back to school by the principal and forced to sit out there and eat anyway. If I skipped school for the day, then I could avoid feeling left out as well as getting in trouble again for walking home. My plan was set.

The week of the picnic I told Laila that I wasn't going because my mom wasn't coming to school to eat with me. She asked if I was sure, that maybe she was coming and just hadn't told me yet. That was Laila, ever hopeful that things weren't going to turn out as bad as they seemed to me. I told her of all the times before when I had something special at school and mom hadn't shown up.

She told me that she still thought that I should come, that she wanted me to meet her mother and she was sure that her mom wouldn't mind if I sat with them. My concern was her mom would say no and I'd still be left to sit alone, and I told her so. She then said she would ask her mother just to make sure, but she was certain that her mother would say yes. I made sure Laila knew that if I didn't have a definite answer about eating with her and her mother I would be staying home that day; no ifs, ands, or buts.

The next day at school Laila walked up to me smiling. The first thing she said when she saw me was that her mother had said yes. She also told me that her mother wanted me to know that I better be at school that day because she wanted to meet this young lady that was causing all this trouble in the classroom and fighting all the time.

What!?! I could not believe it. Laila had told her mother about me. On one hand, I was shocked that she would even talk about me outside of school. On the other, I couldn't believe that she had told her mother of my behavior and not only did she allow her to stay friends with me, but that she also wanted to meet me. I asked Laila why she would tell her mom all of this. She just shrugged her shoulders and then Skye admitted that she'd been telling her mom about things I've done since fourth grade.

I hadn't even known Skye in fourth grade, I only knew of her. I was not aware that she even noticed me enough to tell stories about me. Now I had an entirely different reason to be worried about the picnic. Laila and Skye didn't seem worried about their mothers meeting me, but I was. I thought for sure that I was going to get a dressing down by both of their parents, great!

On the Friday of the picnic all I could think of was my first encounter with their parents. I worried myself silly. When the time finally came both moms met me with smiles. Skye's mother, Ms. Elaine, said that she'd heard a lot about me, mostly not so good things. Laila's mom, Ms. Michelle, chimed in with an agreement and they both started laughing. I was confused. I thought that they were going to be none too happy about meeting me, but they seemed happy to finally be introduced to the child they'd heard so many stories about.

I immediately became relaxed and started being my usual self. While in line to get our food, I asked Ms. Michelle if she'd like another child, I'd definitely be up for a change. She just laughed, hugged me, and said that I was funny. It was a genuine laugh and a genuine hug. Right then I fell in love with Laila's mom.

She may have thought that I was joking. I did say it to be funny and I got the desired result from it, but I was quite serious. I really did wish that I could live in a different family with a different mom. In a way, I loved my mom, I always would. It's just that she didn't get me at all and I could never get from her what I really wanted. What these other mothers seemed to give so freely.

I used to wish all the time that I was adopted and my real parents just lost track of me when they got on their feet. I'd dream that one day they would come back to get me. They'd love me like I saw other parents love on their kids, like Claire Huxtable on "The Cosby Show" loved her children.

I remembered Skye's mom from the chorus performances she would come to. She always hugged on Skye after the event was over, looking at her proudly, lovingly. Everyone's parents were like that and I'd look on, longing to be a part of someone else's family.

When we had gotten our plates Skye and her mother went and sat separate from us on the grass. During lunch, I rattled off a list of benefits that Ms. Michelle would have by taking in a new daughter. All of them were meant to be funny, but silently I was pleading that she would take me seriously. Lunch was fun. I had a great time eating with Laila and her mother, who laughed at just about everything I had to say. I was surprised that a grown up could find me so humorous. Even more so, I was shocked that a parent would sit and listen to what a child had to say, and with real interest in what they were saying.

Mom never did that. She was always half listening. She would either answer with a half-hearted "uh huh" at the end or she would interrupt you and quote some scripture or make a comment that pretty much said that you were talking nonsense.

At the end of lunch, she gave me another hug and told me that I had a great sense of humor and that she liked me. But she didn't let me go from that hug immediately. She continued to hold on to me as she spoke with me about my behavior in school. The way she talked to me brought up so much emotion within me. It was hard to keep from crying, but she spoke to me with love, like she really did care about me.

In the end, when she let me go I was close to tears, but I don't think she noticed. She then asked if I was going to try and do better. I did what I always do to hide my sorrow, inject humor into the situation. I just chuckled and told her I couldn't promise anything. That made her laugh and she threatened to come back up to the school and spank my butt. I told her I'd make sure that I was bad so at least I know I'd see her again. As Laila and I were walking away I turned and told her that I'd experienced worse and I'd welcome her spankings. That was the God's honest truth. I walked away still hearing her laughter behind us.

That day was one of the best days of my life. When I'd have a good day like that, at bedtime I'd replay every detail, over and over in my mind; especially the hugs and the love that was given to me. I'd make up different endings in my mind. But all of them would have the same result; I'd end up going home with her and Laila and live with them forever, happily ever after.

*Priceless Treasures

Life for me is never easy
Simple things are always pleasing
A hug can last a lifetime in my mind
The kind that, in my household, are hard to find
The love of a mother is love from another
A mother who shows love to kids of others
Without judgment, she gives freely
What I would pay for if I had the money, really
She sees me, the real me, beyond all my mess
She sees that love can bring out my best
Real hugs are like treasures that I stow away
Conversations and laughter, I want every day
But I have to settle for a corner in my mind
And when all is quiet, my treasures, I find
I play them back in my head all the time
I smile at them and tears fall in silent lines
No one knows the world I yearn for isn't mine

CHAPTER 23

SINS, CHURCH, FORGIVENESS

When we moved into the apartment complex from my brother's town house there was a church van that came to pick up at the apartments. Every Sunday they would come and my friends who lived there would always go. My brothers' friends would go too so they started going with them. One Sunday, Mom was off from work and she decided that we were all going to go.

After that Sunday, whether Mom went or not we got on that bus and went to church. When Mom came with us, we went to big church, that's what we called the service the adults went to. When Mom wasn't there, we had to go to children's church. It wasn't that bad, but I just didn't like it because it reminded me of history class and I hated history.

We had to memorize all these things that happened in the past and quote scriptures. It wasn't very fun. In Louisiana, we got to go to Vacation Bible School during the summer. That was great because they fed us every day and we got candy and things for memorizing scripture. Plus, we'd play games to help us remember things about God and the Bible. We only got candy every now and then here.

Plus, I was never in class with my friends because you were put in groups by age, not grade. During the summer after fifth grade our Sunday school teacher talked to us a lot about being saved. She told us that as children we didn't have to carry our own sins. But when we turned thirteen all of that would change.

We would start to carry the weight of our own sins then. We would be responsible for everything that we did wrong in God's eyes from then on out. That's why we needed salvation. We had to believe that Jesus died on a cross for our sins. That was the only way we would be forgiven for the things we did wrong.

This information made me dread the day that I would turn thirteen. Because, based on all she said I was doing a great deal of sinning. Most of my sins were kept a secret between me and whoever I participated in them with. At the time, I was glad that God didn't hold my sins against me at the age of twelve, but I only had about a month to get it together.

There were so many things that I had done wrong, was doing wrong, and thought about doing wrong. Even my thoughts were a sin. That summer was when Samantha had come back to stay with my mother and she never really stayed home. She was always gone with her friends or some man. And when she was gone she left for days at a time.

Simeon was always left at home with us. If Samantha was there it would usually be in the daytime. But when she wasn't, I'd always end up watching him. My brothers couldn't be responsible for watching him because they would always forget to feed him or change his diaper. Plus, they spent most of their summer outside with their friends and Simeon couldn't even walk yet.

Mom had her job that she always worked. Even when she would get home she was sometimes too tired to want to watch Simeon. She would always tell me that I had nothing to do all day but sit around the house anyway; it wouldn't hurt me to watch the baby. Mom never really said much to Samantha about leaving Simeon there unless she had been gone for days. Even then her scolding was rather mild, as if she were afraid to really tell Samantha anything.

I spent a lot of time in the house that summer and it wasn't fun. I couldn't do anything that I wanted to do because I had Simeon. It was almost like I had a baby of my own. So much so that later Simeon would start to call me Momma. I hated that and I used to get angry and yell that I wasn't his mom. Sometimes I would get a break though and mom would take him and play with him for a few hours or comb his hair. And at times when Sam was home I didn't have to watch Simeon at all.

But she would always leave at some point, half the time not even letting me know that she was gone. I'd wake up to find only Simeon and I in the house. Or when I'd stay in my room all day one of my brothers would come to the door and tell me they were going outside and Simeon was still in the house. No one knew where Sam had taken off to, but it was mainly my responsibility to watch him when she was gone.

It always seemed like I was the last person to know that she had left. But as soon as my brothers realized she was gone they'd take off before I could leave them there with the baby. They always called my bluff when I'd tell them that I'd leave Simeon in the house by himself. They'd always say, "Oh well," and leave anyway.

I could never bring myself to do that though. I'd be angry, but I knew that if anything ever happened to him I'd lose it. On top of that I think that Sam would have killed me. Even though she wasn't there I knew she loved Simeon in her own way. He'd never lack for anything. She'd always make sure all his food, diapers, and baby things were always well stocked. She kept a separate refrigerator with lots of food just to make sure of it. One that we were never allowed to eat out of no matter that we didn't have any food.

That was another thing that made me angry. I could feed Simeon, but I was never allowed to have any of the food out of that fridge. Simeon was a big baby and he always ate all his food. I would be feeding him while my stomach was growling sometimes, but I'd never eat her food because she'd keep track of how much was there and how much he should be fed.

I took good care of Simeon, but I was also fighting the thoughts that were going through my head. Simeon was about eight months now. I remembered when he was first born and when I would change him I would have to hurry up if his penis was erect because that always meant that he was about to urinate. It would still get that way every now and then, but I guess he had gotten used to his diaper being changed because he would never pee while the diaper was open.

The times that his penis would be erect I would stare at it for a while thinking before I would close the new diaper I had put on him. I wondered if he could get hard and stay that way if I touched him like I'd touched all the other boys. I'd think about it a lot when I'd change or bathe him and it would always come to my mind when we were alone, which happened a lot.

It was like it was on my mind day in and day out. I kept thinking that I shouldn't do it because that would be crossing some invisible line that shouldn't be crossed. I would fight myself about it daily, telling myself all the reasons why it was wrong and why I shouldn't do this. I felt like I was in a constant state of arousal. I would masturbate sometimes up to ten times in one day and would still become aroused within minutes of the last climax.

Eventually, I had made up in my mind that it wouldn't be that bad if I just touched Simeon once, just to satisfy my curiosity, and then I would never do it again. I convinced myself that he was a baby and would be too young to remember it. So, since I was going to do it I should spare him the memory and do it now while he was young.

That day I took him into the bathroom to change his diaper. I locked the door even though no one was there except Karen because I wanted to be sure I wasn't caught. I took his diaper off, cleaned him up, and positioned a new diaper under his bottom all ready to be closed quickly if someone jingled on the door.

When I touched him, it didn't take long for his penis to react. It sprang up immediately. Before I had ever even done anything to him I had already been aroused. When I saw his erection, my arousal intensified. I kept on touching him and started to touch myself at the same time. Even though I was wishing that I wasn't doing this, I was still excited enough to finish.

When I did finish, I felt horrible immediately. I kept silently asking myself, what have I done? I started to cry as I taped his diaper into place and put him on the floor. He was only nine months old. I had violated a baby. I continued to cry as I cleaned myself up and washed my hands, ashamed. What made it worse is that he was making happy noises and crawling around the floor of the bathroom as if nothing had happened.

He was innocent. I never thought that I would stoop so low as to mess with an innocent baby. At that moment, I truly hated myself. I believed myself to be evil if I could do such a thing. I deserved hell. I was thirteen years old and I should've known better.

The next Sunday at children's church I knew what I had to do. There was no way that I would be forgiven of this or any of the other things I had been doing unless I gave my life to Christ. I had to accept Him into my heart so that I could be forgiven.

I told the Sunday school teacher that I wanted to be saved. When she pulled me off to the side I was shaking so badly that she suggested we sit down. I had tears streaming down my face unchecked. We said the prayer together and when it was finished I still could not stop crying. She told me the scripture about confessing your sins so that you could be freed from them.

She then asked if I had something to confess. I had an arsenal of things that I could confess, but I couldn't tell this lady what I had done. I couldn't say any of the things that were on my mind out loud. She would think that I was evil. She would tell me that God couldn't possibly save someone like me. So, instead of confessing the truth of my deepest, darkest sins I confessed that I had been a very bad kid in school. I told her about all the fights and beating up other kids.

She accepted everything I said to be suitable for forgiveness. She then told me that I was saved and that I should live my life the way that God would want me to. Even though I hadn't told her anything I'd really needed forgiveness for, I still felt better. I was a part of God's people now; I could go to God in prayer and ask for forgiveness.

When I went home that's exactly what I did. I went off by myself and asked God to forgive me for everything I had done wrong. My thoughts, my actions, both things that I had done to the innocent and things that I had done with others like me. Afterwards I hoped and prayed that God had forgiven me. I wasn't too sure of it because they were all bad things and I was sure that God had a limit on what He could and could not forgive.

I was told that God would forgive all your sins, but I just didn't think so. I thought for sure that they must be talking about normal sins. To me, normal sins were anything within the Ten Commandments. My sins weren't normal. I wasn't normal.

CHAPTER 24

MY THIRTEENTH BIRTHDAY

Every year for my birthday I would get so excited. All the way up until the day and then I would be depressed. This year was no different. I was a dreamer. I'd always imagine that this year would be different, that this year, Mom would remember my birthday. I'd spend hours thinking about how she would pretend that she'd forgotten, but then she would throw me a surprise party with presents and it would be the best birthday ever.

That never happened. What would make it so bad is that she would remember other siblings' birthdays. Either on her own or someone would remind her, but most times no one remembered my birthday either. Reagan was usually the only one I could count on that wouldn't forget.

Mom had thrown a birthday party for Karen, Derrick, and Daniel before, with the help of other siblings. Come to think of it, it was most likely someone else's idea. They weren't much, but at least she did something. Matthew's birthday didn't count in my mind because she always remembered his. I could never understand it. She had three children's birthdays in the same month, almost within a one week span, and she just couldn't remember mine.

Matthew's birthday came first; Charlie's came three days later, and just three more days after that was mine. By the time my birthday rolled around she always had to be reminded. She made me feel like she didn't really care about me as much as everyone else.

So, I decided that I was not going to say anything to anyone this year. Just to see, I just wanted to see if she would remember. I still had my daydreams about having them surprise me, which never failed. But this time, this time I was going to be more level headed about this thing. I told myself every day that she wasn't going to remember, despite my daydreams I still knew better.

I woke up that morning and didn't say a word to anyone. I went about my day as if it were a normal one. No one said a thing to me. But, like I always do, I thought that since no one was saying anything that something was up. One side of me thought for sure that since I had become a teenager on this day they had decided to surprise me. The other side warned me not to hold my breath.

I realized around eight in the evening what had really happened. They had all forgotten. Every single-family member had forgotten my birthday. I had been sitting on the sofa waiting and nothing had happened so I began to cry. That's when Samantha finally noticed and brought it to my mom's attention that I was crying.

"Girl, what you cryin' for?" Mom said, bewildered that I'd even been sitting there silently crying. Then I told her that it was my birthday and everybody had forgotten. She looked shocked and then went on to tell me that I should've told someone that it was my birthday instead of sitting there crying.

What? Why should I be the one telling anybody anything! That made me cry even more, that she would say something like that to me. Then she said, dismissively, "Well, I forgot, what you want me to do about it?" This was not how I thought this conversation was supposed to go. Her tone implied that I was at fault for this.

I got angry and started wailing through my tears about how she always forgets my birthday every single year. How it amazes me that she can remember everyone else's birthday, even the ones that come days before mine, but never remembered me. That this time no one remembered and that I didn't even get the customary cake this year. I was thirteen years old, that's a special birthday and absolutely no one remembered!

Only then did I think she really recognized how upset I was. She got up from the dining room table where she and Samantha had been sitting and told Samantha, "Come on, let's go to the store and get a cake." For me though, it was too late, I was far past disappointment. Nothing she could do would erase this day and a cake was not going to make up for it.

When she came back I was laying in my bed, still crying. She told me to come out because she had gotten me a special cake this time. Not one that she had to bake herself. It was store bought and decorated. When I came out of my room, sure enough, there sat a cake that had come from the bakery. This was my first ever and it brought just a tad bit of excitement.

It was a very pretty cake, decorated with cream colored icing and red flowers all over it. She did her usual and asked how big of a piece I wanted. She then cut it and gave me my share. I had never seen a cake before that was blood red in the inside. I have had yellow and white cakes, yes, but never red. I've even seen orange before, and I hate carrot cakes.

Apprehension started to rise as I sliced off a chunk with my fork. Everyone was watching me as I put the cake in my mouth. The taste of it didn't match what my mind registered as good, worse than the taste of carrot cake. I turned to my mother and asked what kind of cake it was and she said red velvet. As I swallowed the last bit of it a very bitter after taste surfaced.

She noticed my facial expression and asked what was wrong with it. When I told her, she took a piece for herself and tried it. When she said she found nothing wrong with the cake everyone else took a piece and they all said that it was okay, but I didn't like it at all. I had to wonder if they were saying it just to make me feel better about getting a gross cake on the worst birthday ever.

I turned and left to go back into my room for the night. I didn't stay to see if anyone finished their cake. I knew the truth over the course of that next week though. Had that cake been good I wouldn't have opened the fridge to see it staring back at me every day for a week afterwards. Mom kept attesting that nothing was wrong with the cake and that she just hadn't eaten another slice because she didn't eat sweets like that.

Finally, at the end of the week I took the cake out and tossed it. That was one birthday that I would never forget. It was also one of many nights that I cried for hours until I had fallen asleep. Every time I came across a red velvet cake after that day I remembered my thirteenth birthday. I never tried another piece as a kid.

CHAPTER 25

MIDDLE SCHOOL

It was now almost the beginning of the sixth grade. When Mom went school shopping for me, she constantly complained because she had to go into the plus size women's section to buy my clothes at Wal-Mart. I hated the plus size section because the clothes looked like they were made for old women. Everything had flowers or lace on it. Totally not my style in the least!

What made things worse is that I asked if she could buy my clothes in the boy's section. She had a fit about that, saying I was a girl and I would wear women's clothing. Rachel was with her and, as always, she had to make one of her snide comments about me being happy that I was getting anything at all. She then proceeded to tell me that I was ungrateful and that Mom shouldn't buy me anything. Then she tried to convince Mom not to buy me any clothes.

I knew Mom wouldn't listen to her. I also knew that she did this to shut me up. I ended up getting four or five outfits that were all flower, lace, cotton, and spandex. Things I would never wear, things that my mother had wasted her money to buy. I shoved them all into the back of the closet when I'd gotten home, never to be seen again.

This school year Marie decided to step in with the preparations for school. I liked having Marie around because she was all about school and she made my mother come with her to open house the week before school started.

I was always excited about school and for the first time I'd have the chance to meet with my teachers, get my schedule, and get my school supplies list before school started. I used to hate being one of the only kids in school that didn't bring my school supplies on the first day.

When we got there, we found out that my homeroom class would be upstairs. I hadn't been to a school in years that had more than one floor and I was happy that I'd be upstairs for a change. But this school was different because it had ramps going up and down from the office instead of stairs, which made it so much cooler in my eyes.

When we came into the sixth-grade hallway we took a right, as instructed by the office, we were going to meet Mrs. Steele. She was going to be my homeroom, Language Arts, and Social Studies teacher. There was her name hanging above the doorway. As we walked toward it a Mexican woman appeared in the doorway. At first, I thought it was someone's mother, but then she smiled and reached out her hand toward Marie.

That's when I realized that she was my teacher. I had never seen a Hispanic teacher before. Black teachers were few and far between, but Hispanic teachers were unheard of. What shocked me even more was that she spoke with no accent. If I closed my eyes and listened to her, I would've thought she was a white woman. It was odd.

She ushered us into the room and as she spoke to my sister and Mom I just looked on, amazed. My teacher, my sixth-grade teacher, was Hispanic. In my ignorance, I must admit that I didn't like it. She was telling my mom that she had previously taught Special Education and she was looking forward to teaching regular students that year.

I knew what Special Education was, but I also thought that because she had taught it for most of her teaching career that she may not be capable of teaching other classes. I judged her based on her race and her previous teaching skills. I was not happy at all about being in her classroom for the year. She also spoke with me for a few minutes, but I didn't say much. I wasn't happy with this situation at all.

We also met the other teacher on the team, Ms. Wells. I remember thinking that it would have been better had I at least had her as my homeroom teacher, as if that would up my status with other students. Ms. Wells was a white, young teacher with blonde hair. I was used to having white teachers, but none so young and pretty. I remember being angry because I didn't have her for homeroom.

On the first day of school I found out that Skye was also in my homeroom class. I was so happy to see her, but sad to see that Laila was on a different team. We didn't get to talk much in school because all our classes were different. I wanted Laila's phone number, but instead of asking her I dared her to give it to me. I went at it the roundabout way because I didn't want to get my feelings hurt if I asked and she told me no. But she gave it to me with no hesitation at all.

In the first week of school I began to feel differently about Mrs. Steele. I soon realized that she was just like any other teacher, she just looked different. She was very nice and I liked being in her class because she did things a little differently. She had petitioned the school a year before to make a nature trail in the woods adjacent to it and she took us on a walk through it to show us where it was and what her plans were for the trail.

While she was speaking, a boy started picking at me, saying little unpleasant remarks about me being fat. On our walk back to the school I got angry and did what I do best. I had to establish who I was so that this didn't start a trend with other students thinking that they could pick on me. I stopped dead in the middle of the trail and loudly cussed him up one side and down the other.

Mrs. Steele stopped walking, turned and came back towards me. The first thing she asked was if I was okay. She didn't yell at me, she didn't send me to the office, she didn't even look angry at what I'd said. When I told her what happened she simply said that I shouldn't give other people the power to make me angry because once I show it, they've won.

She then proceeded to take the boy to the front of the line and said not one more word to me. I was speechless. What she said made a lot of sense even though what she did about the situation didn't. I was used to being punished and I had been ready for it, but it never came. She never sent me to the office or wrote me up for it. That gained her a lot of respect in my eyes, so much so that I never acted out in her classroom, ever again.

I couldn't say the same for other teachers though. They all seemed to carry the same attitude that most of my other teachers had. Like they don't really care for you, they're just here to do a job. I'd get in trouble in other classes a lot. If someone picked on me I'd cuss them out or beat them up and get sent to the principal's office. If I didn't like a teacher and he or she did something I didn't like I'd cuss at them.

I would get detention or in-school suspension left and right. Mrs. Steele would always seem surprised to see me sitting in ISS or detention after school. That's if I even went to detention. Mom didn't have a car and this school wasn't within walking distance, so when I got detention I'd get on the bus anyway and then end up having it converted to in-school suspension because of it.

Mrs. Steele would come and visit me in ISS during lunch sometimes. She just couldn't get over how good I was in her classroom, but how bad I was with everyone else. But she'd never get angry with me. She always seemed like she was trying to understand the inner workings of me, rather than judging me on my behavior.

Once, when Ms. Wells was absent, we had a substitute named Mrs. Matthews. She was the nicest lady, but something about her irked me. She talked to us as if we were in kindergarten and she was still writing our names on the board when we did something bad. She had quite a few names on the board. Surprisingly, mine wasn't one of them.

The same boy from the beginning of the year took that moment to start picking at me again. So, I whispered some unpleasant comments right back to him. I said something that made him really angry, and to retaliate, he called me a bitch. Immediately, I saw red. That was automatically the worse thing he could've said to me.

As fast as if it were a reflex I picked up the desk I was sitting at and sent it sailing across the back of the room and hit him dead on. I'd thrown it with enough force to knock him out of his seat and onto the floor under the thrown desk. He lay stunned for a split second and then jumped up and ran straight for me, crouching as if to tackle me down like a football player.

I quickly moved to one side and let him slam into the wall. Instantly, I jumped on top of him, grabbed his shirt front, and punched him repeatedly. I was in such a rage that I don't remember what happened after that. All I remember is the substitute screaming and that she never substituted another class that I was in for the rest of that year.

CHAPTER 26

SEX EDUCATION

I had my first sex education class in fourth grade. I learned that the stuff coming out of Daniel's penis was called sperm and if it got inside the vagina it's what caused women to get pregnant. I already knew that women and men got together to have sex and sometimes women got pregnant because of it, but I didn't know that men put this stuff inside a woman's vagina so that she might conceive.

I was thirteen years old and in the sixth grade when Daniel started asking me if he could put his penis in my vagina. Well, his way of saying it was "let me stick it in". Even the way he said it made it sound gross. It seemed like every time we did something together I was grossed out at some point. I thought it was very nasty that he would even ask to do such a thing.

I had gotten saved, yes, but the urges had not magically gone away. The next time I was approached by Daniel I told him that I'd gotten saved and that I didn't want to do this anymore. He told me his usual, okay, but just this once. It's not like I didn't want to so I went ahead and did it anyway. I couldn't seem to make myself dislike the hunching.

As for him putting his penis in my vagina, I flat out said no and let my disgust of it show. That still didn't faze him because every time we would hunch he would start off by asking me if he could do it. If I was going to continue to do this I wanted boundaries to what extent we would go with it and he just didn't seem to understand that.

I'd learned in church that God wanted you to remain a virgin until you got married. That it was something special that you saved to give to your spouse on your wedding night. That's what I wanted to do. If I could not be good and save myself totally, I at least wanted that to be left for my husband, the man I would love.

I thought about love a lot. I absolutely loved music. All kinds of music, but what I loved the most were songs by Brian McKnight. I used to daydream about him a lot. That one day he would see me and just fall in love with this broken person. That he would marry me, and love me right, and I'd turn into a good person. I just knew that based on his songs, he knew a lot about love and he'd be the one to teach me the right way to love.

I first fell in love with him because of one song called "One Last Cry", it said everything to me. I felt like he understood me on a level that no one else could. I knew the song was about a woman he loved, but to me, it crossed over into something different. That I would just sit down and have one last cry about all the things that happened to me and all the things I'd done and then I'd leave it all behind.

But that never happened. I remained in the care of my

mother with Daniel and Simeon and my nephews who were there from time to time. Brian McKnight never came to save me; he would always remain in my dreams.

Those were very aggravating times for me. I just couldn't understand why Daniel wouldn't drop the subject and leave it alone. I'd always encourage him to go get a girlfriend so that he could do stuff like that with her. He was sixteen years old and had never had a girlfriend. He blamed the reason on Derrick, saying that the girls always liked Derrick more.

This was true. Even if they had met Daniel first, eventually they would meet Derrick and all interest in Daniel went out the window. Daniel would become livid when this would happen and try to fight Derrick. He'd end up getting even angrier in the end because he couldn't beat Derrick up. Daniel was tall and lanky while Derrick was shorter, stockier, and more athletic.

But I don't think that's what kept all the girls' attention. Daniel was just plain weird. He would always try to crack jokes and do weird things in front of my friends that just weren't funny. All the girls would always ask me why he was so weird and I'd just say I didn't know. A lot of times they would even use the word creepy when describing him.

Aside from my issues with Daniel, I continued to have the urge to touch Simeon. Every time I'd fall into it and do it again I would go through the same deep depression and guilt process over it. But eventually I would get around to doing it again. It was a cycle that I couldn't break, didn't know how to.

I couldn't figure out what was so wrong with me that I just couldn't let it go and leave him alone.

I'd try to fight it but I'd come back with the same excuses; that he wouldn't remember it, he must like it if he doesn't cry when I do it, it's not hurting him. Then afterwards I would call myself every disgusting name I could think of. I'd cry every time asking myself what I could have been thinking. On some level, I knew that even if I wasn't hurting him physically it was still affecting him negatively.

By this time, Mom would constantly tell me that I was going to hell because I listened to so many different types of secular music, especially rap with all its foul language. I'd always think that she didn't know the half of it. If I could go to hell just for listening to music, then Satan would put me under the fiery coals for what I was doing.

Even though I knew that I was hell bound. I still prayed every night and asked for forgiveness. I'd think that if I died in my sleep then at least God might have actually forgiven me for everything I'd done and since I was sleeping I wasn't sinning. That meant that I could die with a clean heart.

I'd also pray, with tears streaming down my face, that God would take me in my sleep or that He could kill me somehow. That someone would do a drive-by or just decide that I wasn't fit to live on this earth and just shoot me. I really felt that I wasn't fit to live. Most of the people living on earth were better people than I was.

On the other hand, I was also angry with God. I didn't have a choice in whether He created me or not, He should've just left me where I was, unknown to this world. I would always wish that I didn't exist, that I was nothing. I felt like He put me here and then had the gall to tell me that I couldn't decide to take my own life because He would definitely send me to hell. That's what Mom said anyway. Something about "whoever takes his life will lose it."

I used to think up different ways to kill myself. I'd wonder if I asked for forgiveness right before I pulled the trigger, cut myself, or swallowed loads of pills if God would truly forgive me and let me in. One thing I knew for sure, beyond the shadow of a doubt, was that I wasn't worthy. Even though I believed and had gotten saved, I still was nowhere near worthy.

I didn't know how to fix myself so I continued to fall. Not only in the sense that I kept on sinning, but every day was far more depressing than the one before it. I gave up on even trying to stop doing the things that I was doing to Simeon. And whenever I felt like we could get away with it and I felt the urge, I would seek Daniel out.

There was only one thing that I couldn't give into and that was having sexual intercourse with my own brother. I couldn't bring myself to want to do that, no matter how many times he tried. In some ways, I felt I still had a chance to save myself from going to hell if I could just stop the things that I was doing, if I could just be good. But having sex with him would be the one thing that I couldn't bounce back from. He just couldn't understand that I didn't even have a desire to do that, in the least.

Sometimes during church service the pastor would say that God will forgive you for any wrong, that it doesn't matter what it is. So, I'd ask for forgiveness, but I didn't know what to do to keep myself from falling again. One day I decided that if I told on Daniel to Mom that he would stop.

I thought he might be angry at me for telling when I was at fault at times too, but I thought if she were watching us it would make the difference. I didn't feel threatened by what Dad would do about it now because he lived miles and miles away. I didn't have anything to fear from him.

So, I told her that Daniel kept messing with me. When she'd ask me what I meant, I'd tell her in a nasty way. I just couldn't describe to her the things that we'd been doing. But she would ask what I meant by that and I'd just repeat that it was in a nasty way. I didn't feel like I should have to tell her what exactly went on. She should know what that meant and do something about it.

But all she ever did, out of the three or four times I told her over the years, was tell him, "Daniel, you better stop messing with that girl." It reminded me of those times she'd told me, "You better stop doing that," when the school would call her about my behavior. It never really did anything, but made Daniel angry. We'd stop for a while after that, but eventually it would start back up again.

CHAPTER 27

ONE AWESOME QUARTER

The excitement of being in school again was over. There was always a period of time that I couldn't wait to go to school, being happy that I was finally in school again, and then hating that I had to go to school. I lost my zeal for it a lot earlier that year.

I wasn't getting that much sleep sometimes because of Simeon. He'd fight every night that I had him because he didn't want to go to sleep. So, I couldn't just go to sleep on him no matter how tired I was. He was walking and getting around well enough now to get into things. I had to stay up with him until he finally wound down and went to sleep. This was about eleven or twelve at night.

Our bus came at around six thirty in the morning and we had to be up and out the door by six twenty because we had a long walk to our bus stop. All this meant that I had to get up at about five fifty, feeling like I had just gotten to sleep. I spent a lot of days feeling like a zombie at school.

It was also very hard for me to do my homework after school because I was the type of child that needed absolute silence to concentrate. I'd always have a difficult time because my brothers would come home and turn on the cartoons as soon as we got there. I had tried to do my homework in my room, but would end up falling asleep. So, I needed to be at the kitchen table with complete silence to get it done.

That almost never happened and when there was a lot of noise it would take me double and sometimes triple the normal time it takes to do homework. It all depended on if I had to read. I was never made to multi-task. I could not comprehend what I was reading if there was noise going on at the same time.

I'd ask my brothers to turn the television off, but they'd always say no. They were of the attitude that I was just being obnoxious. That, if they could do their homework with the TV on, then so could I. I'd tell my mom and she'd say something to them, but she was always at work when we came home. She was never the type to really make anyone do anything so they didn't fear her even if she had said she would punish them, which she never did.

Eventually, I got tired and I quit. The only subject I kept up with was my math because I loved math. And luckily, I almost never had homework in Science. I pretty much kept a good grade average in Ms. Wells' classes. I can't say the same thing for Mrs. Steele's classes though.

Most times I slept through Social Studies, which was the most draining part of the day for me. In Language Arts, I half-heartedly did the work. The only time I really did my best is when she would let us write about anything that we wanted to. I loved to write and I'd eagerly do that assignment.

I had the worst grade in Social Studies because I'd sleep almost every day. The only times that I was awake for this class was when we had open discussions. She'd always pick some topic to discuss in current affairs and the whole class would get involved and weigh in their opinion. Lots of times it was controversial and you'd have half the class agreeing while the other half didn't.

I'd always sit and think on it for a while and then make a comment. That's how Mrs. Steele figured it out. She pulled me aside one day and told me that she knew that I was smart because of my writing and during class discussions my comments always had a depth to them that would silence the class and make them think for a moment before the discussions would continue.

During her conversation with me she asked why I never turned in my homework and why I slept every day in her class. I told her why along with the fact that I hated Social Studies because it was boring. She talked to me about the importance of education and that I was smart enough to finish high school and go to college. That, if I started now with making good grades, by the time I finished high school I could have colleges paying for me to go to their schools.

In all my years, no one had ever told me that I was smart enough to go to college, let alone that my grades could be the key to it. Reagan was the only child in our family who always made straight A's. She was really smart and always reading. I had told Mrs. Steele so. What struck me was that she'd said I was fully capable of doing the exact same thing.

I couldn't believe that she'd told me that. Book wise, Reagan was the smartest one in our family; it was like blasphemy when Mrs. Steele told me that I was just as smart as her. To this day, the siblings of this family still call Reagan "The Information Lady", a nickname we'd dubbed her in our childhood because she usually had the answer to a question we had.

Mrs. Steele had gotten me to thinking, but it wasn't the type of thinking that usually happened after a conversation like that. My thoughts were full of doubts. I didn't think she really knew what she was saying. There's no way that I could be that smart. There's no way that I could be that dedicated. That's what I worried about the most.

Within days of that conversation Marie had taken a trip to Louisiana and came back with some things we had left behind at my father's house. One of those things was a folder that all my awards and achievements had been kept in. It contained my certificates for being a straight A honor roll student, perfect attendance, and so on. Even though I had repeated grades, I had always made straight A's. These things reminded me of how well I used to do in school and still did at times in fourth and fifth grade in Georgia.

I was so excited that I compiled all my awards from Louisiana and Georgia into one folder and brought them to school to show Mrs. Steele. Karen's honor roll ribbons were also included because I saw them as mine now. I didn't give a second thought to the fact that I had stolen them and I was misrepresenting myself by showing them to her.

I was nervous about giving her that folder at first. I didn't know whether she would even take the time out to see what I wanted to show her. I didn't want her to look at them as my mother did and just say, "Uh huh." I would have been crushed if she had.

But all my nervousness had been for nothing. Her face lit up when I presented her with my folder of awards. She was excited to see that I had so many. She actually kept them at her desk during class and took the time to look through them while I surreptitiously watched from my desk. I stayed awake that entire day wondering what she was thinking. I cataloged every smile she displayed to my brain as she turned from one award to the next. I would think about them later, the smiles, and come up with one of my usual scenarios of how she would adopt me and raise me as her own because she thought I was so smart.

At the end of the day she called me to the side while everyone was getting ready to go. She told me how nice it was that I shared them with her and told me that she wished I'd do the same things in her class. I told her that I would if she'd just adopt me. As always, I appeared humorous but I was quite serious in my own mind. If she could take me away I was quite sure I could make those A's and get that scholarship to college.

From then on out it was my goal to get her to adopt me.

While I knew it wasn't plausible in the real world, it was nice to daydream about.

One day she brought pictures to school to show us the garden that she had at home. She wanted us to see what she would like to plant out on the nature trail and how beautiful it would look if she could get the approval to do it. She wanted to make something out there that could be used in the Science classes as well.

While viewing the pictures, all I could think of is the huge house that was in the background of all those pictures. Her house looked even bigger than my father's house. I began to tease and say that that was my house and I lived with Mrs. Steele, that she'd adopted me. All the students that were surrounding us and Mrs. Steele began to laugh.

When everyone dispersed, I told her that I used to live in a big house before too. I told her about my dad's house and why we didn't live there anymore and how I missed the house, but I didn't miss my father. The conversation had turned serious pretty quickly. I then looked her in the eye and told her seriously that if she would adopt me and let me come to live with her, I'd give her the straight A's that she wanted. She just smiled at me and said she was sure that I would.

It was the end of the second nine weeks of school. A few days later she was handing out report cards with grades on them that I didn't much care to look at. I'd get sad when I'd see my grades because I'd always have the feeling that I could've done better if I just had some place quiet to study at home, got enough sleep at night, and most popular; lived with

Laila and her mom or Mrs. Steele.

After handing out all the report cards she called me to her desk while everyone got ready to leave. She told me that she'd thought about what I had said the other day over the weekend. While she couldn't adopt me, what she could do was let me have a slumber party at her house one weekend. The catch was that I had to make all A's for the third nine weeks we were starting.

I was amazed; awed that she would even think about me while she was living her own life at home and that she would offer me something so personal. Excited at the prospect I answered immediately. She laughed at my giddiness, but I didn't care. I was just short of dancing.

That excitement faded when I got home with the television playing loudly, Simeon at my side pestering me with his baby gibberish, and my mom's disappointment of coming home and me not having the apartment spotless. Admittedly, Marie and some of my other siblings had listened to my plight. They had gotten my mother to implement a plan for all of us to have a scheduled cleaning day, but I no longer cared. I was burnt out on doing anything around the house except for cleaning up after myself and washing my own clothes. So, when it was my day to clean the dishes it almost never got done.

I had gotten tired of it all because no matter what I did Mom always found fault with it. I felt like if she was going to fuss at me anyway, I might as well give her reason to. All of these things were like a weight on me as soon as I came home. There was no way I was going to be able to accomplish what Mrs. Steele was asking, especially with PE on my schedule. I hated PE because the rule was that we had to dress out in front of all the other girls. I'd always get in trouble for dressing in the bathroom stalls. Sometimes I didn't dress out at all just so I wouldn't have to butt heads with the coach.

The next day I spoke with Mrs. Steele about it. I had awakened that morning with renewed purpose, maybe we could compromise. She politely listened to everything I had to say about the subject, smiled, and then told me no. That if I was going to do this I had to be all in. I begged her a few more times but it did not shake her resolve.

I had a very hard time being frustrated with her because she was smiling and I could tell that my plan to get her to compromise was humorous to her. In turn, it made me smile and laugh even though my pleas were earnest.

After seeing that I couldn't sway her I just sighed dramatically and walked away, but I walked away smiling. In the end, she just told me that if I tried my best I would do it. My mindset was, okay, I'll show her. I'll try my best and when it doesn't happen she'll see that my life is too hard to accomplish what she's asking.

So, every day I dressed out for PE and tried my best to run, play, and exercise. I paid attention in every class and did my best not to fall asleep. I went home and through endless hours of cartoons, the baby, and Mom nagging; finished my homework. It was extremely hard at times, but I stuck to it just for the slim chance that I might succeed. I didn't want to miss out on the opportunity to be somewhere nice, even if it were only for a couple of days. The point was that it wasn't home, the place I never wanted to be.

Finally, the quarter ended and all the grades were in. I watched Mrs. Steele's face as she passed out everyone's report cards. She had a very sober look about her that made me feel like she knew that I didn't make it. So, I sat there preparing myself for the worst. I just knew that it couldn't be good news.

She'd given out all the report cards except mine. She called me to her desk with a very serious expression on her face. When I got there, she did not smile, she just gave me my report card and told me to open it. Out of all my classes, I just knew I had gotten a B in PE. I felt fairly strong about all but that one class.

Slowly, I opened the envelope and pulled out the report card. When I unfolded it, I could not believe my eyes. I had gotten an A in every single subject, even PE. My mouth sat open in amazement, my eyes boggled at what they saw. I had done it and when I looked back at her she had one of those warm, loving smiles, the kind I keep locked inside of my dream box.

She looked at me like I had seen proud parents look at their children and quietly said, "Congratulations, you did it." She stood to hug me briefly and I awkwardly hugged her back. I didn't get hugs often and getting one from a teacher felt even more awkward. But I could feel the wealth of delight she had in what I'd accomplished. All I wanted to know after that was whether she was going to make good on her end of the bargain. I was concerned because sometimes people didn't keep their word.

Softly, out of earshot of the rest of the class, she discussed the details of the slumber party. It wasn't going to be as big as she had planned because her husband, who was an accountant, was studying to take an extremely important test and we couldn't make a lot of noise.

I was allowed to invite three of my friends. She wanted us to be able to leave the house so that he could study on Saturday so she had put a limit on the number of friends I could bring. The sleepover would happen the very next Friday so that I would have time to invite them. After everything was clarified, she asked if I was okay with everything. Of course, I was!

It was a given, as far as who I invited to come. It didn't matter that I had a limit because there were only two people that I really wanted to go in the first place. The sad part about it was that Laila couldn't go; her family had already made plans for that weekend. Skye was as excited as I was though because she was also in Mrs. Steele's class.

I was trying my best to find two more people, but it was hard. Some parents thought it was weird that a teacher wanted children to sleep over at her house. Some of the girls also said no because they didn't want to sleep over at a teacher's house, they thought it was lame. Skye and I didn't care though, this was our teacher and we loved being in her class.

I finally got a third person, Monique, to go at the last minute. The very same girl that had been so snooty to me in third grade ended up living in the same apartment complex that Mom had moved to. She had turned out not to be so bad after all. Her mom had said yes the day before we were set to sleep over.

That Friday we all brought our packed sleepover bags to school. It had been decided by Mrs. Steele and the other parents that it would be easier for her to just leave from school with us in tow instead of picking us up from our individual homes.

I had told Mom about the sleepover and why because she'd also thought that it was strange for a teacher to want students to come over to her house. I can admit, she was a little concerned, but after talking to Mrs. Steele over the phone she agreed to it. From then on out, as usual, I made my own decisions and since everyone else was leaving from school with Mrs. Steele, I decided to do the same.

After school on Friday it only took a short while for the awkwardness of being with Mrs. Steele outside of school to wear off. She was a normal adult when not at school. She let her hair down, so to speak, and we had lots of fun. We had so many choices of what we wanted to eat for dinner and I was excited about the prospects because it wasn't often that I ate out. She was surprised that I had decided on McDonald's and wouldn't budge from my decision.

She'd called out several restaurants; most of them full

service, which I had never set foot inside. I was excited just to have McDonald's. Skye and Monique agreed with me even though Mrs. Steele tried to sway them. She asked me why I wouldn't consider going to a nicer restaurant and I told her that I'd only ever been to McDonald's and Ryan's.

Not believing what I'd just said, she asked me if I was sure I'd never been someplace different. I said that I hadn't and she just looked on ahead through the windshield. I could tell that she was speechless.

So, we had our McDonald's amidst girlish giggles and various topics. Afterwards we went to the movie rental place and got a few movies. When we pulled up to her house three pairs of eyes looked on in amazement at what we saw. Mrs. Steele had a huge house. There were bushes and plants and flowers everywhere. She had 2 full floors and a garage with two basement rooms on the bottom. It was the biggest house I'd ever had the opportunity to go inside.

She pulled up to a two-car garage and opened her side by pressing a button. She showed us the exercise room on the other side of the stairs in the garage and then we grabbed our things and went up to the first floor. On this floor, she had a kitchen that was also big enough for a table and four chairs with space left over, bathroom, laundry room, dining room, living room, entryway and front door, formal living room, and a huge bedroom that we put our stuff down in.

She took us upstairs where there were three more bedrooms, a hall bathroom, and a master bedroom. It boggled our minds how much space she had in this house and it was only her, her husband Bill whom we met in the office they'd made from a spare bedroom, and one daughter who still lived at home. Her other daughter was in college and only came home occasionally.

By the time we came back down to the first floor we felt like we were lost and we told her so. She just laughed and seemed amazed herself that we'd never seen a place so big before. I think that baffled her mind just as much as her house did ours. We had a hard time figuring out where we were in reference to all the different places she'd shown us and they were all in one house.

We settled down to watch movies while Bill stayed upstairs studying. We took turns taking baths while Mrs. Steele stayed downstairs chatting with us. Afterwards she told us we could stay up as long as we wanted and asked where we'd like to sleep. We all agreed that the living room suited us just fine. I felt like sleeping in one of her bedrooms would be too fine for me. I didn't say it out loud, though I wondered if Skye and Monique felt the same way.

She asked if we were sure, she seemed surprised that we didn't want to sleep in a bed. Finally, she gave up, said goodnight and went upstairs. I remember us having a lengthy conversation about how big the house was and that our teacher lived in such a huge place.

Eventually, Skye and Monique went to sleep after we spent hours talking and giggling. I stayed up long after that though, partially because of the grandfather clock that chimed the hours away, but mostly because of all the thoughts that went through my mind.

I thought about how nice the day had been and I went through it all over again in my mind, smiling at all the good memories I had to keep. I thought about how many rooms she had there and how great it would be to live in a place that was so nice and quiet. Aside from the clock, it was peaceful here. I wondered what Mrs. Steele had been thinking when she had become quiet at times during the day after I'd said something. I finally fell asleep dreaming of what it would be like to live there permanently.

The next day she asked how we all slept. I told her that I hadn't slept very well because of the clock. She asked why I hadn't gone over and stopped it. I wouldn't have dreamed of touching something that looked so expensive. I expressed that to her and she brought me over to show me how easy it would've been to stop it. Astounded that she thought it so simple, I told her that I would never touch her clock.

She didn't understand. It amazed me that she had such nice towels in the bathroom and they weren't just for show. I'd never seen things that were so valuable before. I felt like I was walking through some fine museum from the first step I'd taken into her house. I wouldn't dream of touching anything and I'd think twice about it even if she had told me to. When I expressed that to her she blew it off like it was utter nonsense.

After breakfast, we went outside. She had asked us the day before if we would wash her van if she paid us. I was so thankful for what she'd done for me already that I would've washed it for free. Both Skye and I told her so and she'd said she wouldn't dream of having us clean for free when this was supposed to be a fun weekend.

So, we went outside and washed her van while she dug weeds out of her garden. When we were finished, I told Skye that I was going to take the hose and spray Mrs. Steele with it. Immediately Skye went wide eyed and told me not to do it. She was afraid that I'd ruin the weekend if I made Mrs. Steele angry, but I just couldn't resist.

Nervously, Skye called her over so that she could look over the van to make sure that we were done. The instant that she was close enough I sprayed her with the hose and said, "Oh, I'm sorry, I didn't see you there." My facial expression gave it away though. Her face went from shock to determination in two seconds flat and she immediately gave chase after me.

Astonished that she would chase me I quickly dropped the hose, screamed, and started running away. I wasn't quick enough though as I felt water spray across my back. When I turned around Monique and Skye were screaming because she was chasing them with the hose.

They gained ground on her, and as I went to retrieve the bucket we'd used to wash the van, they wrestled the hose from her and came back around the van to where I was. We filled up the bucket while she hid on the other side. Skye and Monique went one way with the hose while I went the other with a full bucket of water. When she came my way, I doused her completely with the entire bucket.

"Looks like you're under attack," Bill said coming out of the garage. I was a bit uneasy upon seeing him because he was supposed to be studying and I must have interrupted him with my antics. I didn't know what was going to happen next. Other than Rachel, I was only ever really afraid of men. In my opinion, they held all the power. They had power to hurt, to withhold, and to take all the fun out of life. I was never truly comfortable when a man was present.

But that wasn't the case with Bill. Mrs. Steele continued to laugh as she explained what I had done. He smiled and said he liked me because I had guts and that she had needed to be drenched, teasing that she had not taken a shower the night before. She asked if we'd disturbed him. He said that he'd been about to come down for lunch anyway when he heard the commotion going on outside and looked out the window from upstairs.

After that we all went inside to change and eat lunch. When we were finished Mrs. Steele gave us ten dollars each, ten whole dollars apiece for washing the van. We were all excited and thought that we'd basically got paid for having fun, it was awesome.

She decided to take us out for a drive and we ended up at the mall. We looked around at a lot of different things and Skye and Monique spent their money while we were there. When Mrs. Steele asked if there was a special store or item I was looking to spend my money on I told her no. She asked what I was going to do with my money and I said that I was going to keep it. I told her that I didn't get this much money often and I wanted to save it and make sure I spent it on something I really wanted.

Again, she looked at me thoughtfully and said okay even though she asked me a few more times afterward if I was sure I didn't want to spend my money. I was quite sure. The mall seemed like a very expensive place. If you bought just one item you would have absolutely no money left and I didn't see anything I wanted that badly.

I had a lot of fun that weekend. It was nice to see the person behind the teacher title. Mrs. Steele was one of those teachers who really cared about students and their well-being. This time I had gone home excited to tell all about the weekend I'd had. When I told my mom all she had to say was, "Uh huh". For some reason, I'd expected a different answer. I'd told her about everything except getting money, but none of it seemed of any interest to her.

I went back to school for that last quarter asking Mrs. Steele if I could sleep over again if I made straight A's this time also. She told me that the first time she'd given me an incentive just to see if I would do it. Now that she knew that I could, she wanted me to make the grades because I wanted to. She wanted me to have the drive to succeed no matter what was going on around me.

Because of this, I didn't try as hard as I should have. Being over at her place was my equivalent of having a small piece of heaven. If I couldn't have that, then what was I working for? I didn't want to totally disappoint her though so I stayed awake in class and did most of my homework. At the end of the year I made mostly A's and B's and passed on to the seventh grade.

CHAPTER 28

EXPERIENCING NEW THINGS

I had a really good friend named Aquila who lived in the apartment above us. She was my best friend in our neighborhood. Even though she was a grade or two above me, we were the same age. She was almost never allowed to come outside. She always had to watch her younger siblings because her mom was always gone. There were rumors that her mom was on drugs, but I never asked her about it.

We were alike in a lot of ways because we both held a lot of responsibility at home. And like me, she didn't have much control over her siblings. The only difference is she would scream at them all the time to try and get them to listen. You could hear her from our apartment. I almost never screamed because they never listened anyway, her siblings or mine.

When we did have a phone, I would talk to her for hours. On the rare times that she could come out we'd always be together, sometimes with some of the other girls from the apartment complex. It's funny that most of us pretty much had the same responsibilities at home, but for different reasons. Some of our parents worked very long hours, some liked to go out and party with friends, and others had an addiction.

Aquila had a little sister named Imani. We were in the same grade but at first, I didn't like her very much because she had a smart mouth. One day walking home from elementary school she cussed me out and said that I thought I was all big and bad, but she could beat me up. She started a fight with me and I beat her up. I had pulled her hair during the fight and a bunch of her braids came out.

Everyone was laughing at her until Aquila came outside. That was the first time I met her and what I didn't know was that if anyone messed with Aquila's little sister or brothers she would beat them up. I heard that in whispers as she approached. I was getting ready for the fight of my life because, as she was coming, Imani bragged that her sister never lost a fight and that she was going to get me.

Everyone had backed out of her way and as soon as she was in earshot, Imani tattled that I'd pulled all her weave out. Aquila then looked to me and asked why I had done it and I told her what Imani had done to start it all. When everyone agreed, she told Imani that she should never have started the fight. She fussed at her and told her to pick her weave up off the sidewalk and go inside.

From then on out Aquila and I were friends. At age thirteen I had another reason why I never became good friends with Imani. We had all played house once and Aquila had made Imani and I the mom and dad, she wanted to be the baby.

Imani had brought me into their room and locked the door and said that we were going to have sex. I laughed at first, thinking that she was playing, but when I laid down like she told me to, she got on top of me. Then we had an argument because I was supposed to be the daddy, which meant I should be on top.

She finally gave in and I laughed and told her out loud some things I'd heard men say to women on the scrambled porn videos while I playfully lay on top of her. Then things started happening in earnest and we ended up hunching each other while Aquila whined on the outside of the door like a baby. When we were almost done, she started banging on the door and asking what we were really doing because we weren't answering her.

Imani kept yelling that we were having sex so she should go away. When we finished, I hurried to open the door and she stepped in. She looked at us funny, but she didn't say anything. From then on I avoided Imani because she would try to sit in my lap or touch and hug me in public, the way a girl would with a boy.

I didn't want anybody to think weird things about me even though I had liked what we did, so I stayed away from her. Plus, she was very aggressive with what she wanted and I didn't like that one bit. I felt that, if I let her, she'd do whatever she wanted, no matter who was watching. I always kept her at a distance.

That same year Monique and I had a mutual friend named Ashley. Ashley had some classes with us, but she also had special education classes. I never really knew why because she seemed normal to me. Once, she asked if I would sleep over at her house. I told her I wouldn't come unless Monique could come also. We'd had so much fun at Mrs. Steele's that I thought we'd have just as much fun sleeping at a friend's house.

Monique's mom got her friend to drop us off at Ashley's house after school on a Friday. When Ashley's mom came home we were surprised that she only gave a vague, uninterested greeting and went straight to her room. An hour or so later she came downstairs dressed for a night on the town, gave Ashley a wad of cash, and told her to order some pizza and whatever else we wanted for the weekend and she left.

I thought it was awesome that her mom had left so much money, but Monique didn't seem to like it. She ended up calling her mom saying that it was boring there and that she wanted to go home. Her mom was out also and told her she would have to wait until the next day. So, we ordered pizza and watched movies until late at night. Ashley had every movie channel on cable, she had the latest video game system, and even though they lived in an apartment, it was a very nice one.

When we went upstairs to her room to go to bed her sheets smelled strongly like urine. Monique got in the bed with her, but I slept on the floor. Oddly, I thought that for sure if I smelled it Monique did too, but she got in the bed anyway.

The next morning Monique's mother came to get her, she asked if I wanted to go home too since we stayed in the same apartment complex, but I told her no. This was still better than being at home to me. After she left, Ashley and I walked to the store and bought loads of junk food and soda and lugged it all back to the apartment.

We ate Doritos for breakfast, it was great. I laid down on the floor facing the TV and started playing her video game. The next thing I knew, she was straddling my butt. I didn't pay her any mind for a while. It didn't bother me that she was there. I just giggled and kept playing.

Then she started grinding her private part up against my butt and I started to get angry. I told her to stop and, when she didn't listen to me, I reached behind my back, grabbed her neck, slammed her on the floor and angrily shouted "Stop!" After that she went to sit on the sofa and I continued playing Sonic.

When I got tired of playing the video game I got up and apologized to her and told her that I don't like to play like that. I only play with boys like that. Then she told me about this one boy in school that she'd lost her virginity to. I asked her a lot of questions about what it was like and how it felt. After she answered all of them she told me to follow her.

We went upstairs to her mother's room, who hadn't come home since Friday night. She asked me if she showed me something would I promise not to beat her up. I told her sure, if she didn't touch me or show me her body parts. It's not that I wouldn't have wanted to do anything; it's just that I didn't like Ashley in that way. A lot of her teeth were crooked and very yellow, she didn't seem like a very clean girl, and I didn't like the smell of her room. It made me feel like she was strongly lacking in the cleanliness department..

After I agreed, she turned on her mother's television and pressed play on the VCR. Immediately a very graphic image of a naked woman popped up and a temporarily fully dressed man was doing some things I'd never seen before to her. My eyes were glued instantly, but then she turned it off. We went back and forth for a bit until I promised her that I was fully capable of stopping the tape exactly where her mom had had it before.

I was a pro at things like this. I'd never seen a porno, but I'd watched some rated R movies before and I knew how to check the timing on a certain scene and go back to it when no one else was around. So, she rewound the entire tape and started from the beginning. She lay on the bed and tried to get me to get up there with her but I said no.

When I laid on the floor she tried to come down there with me, again I told her no. I wanted to be where she couldn't see me and I didn't want to see her. I wanted to focus all my attention on what I saw without interruption or worrying about someone watching me while I watched. I watched that entire movie from beginning to end, eyes absolutely glued to the TV screen, feeling more aroused than

I'd ever been in my life.

Some things I didn't care for, but I only had to watch for a few minutes before it would change to something else. There were all different kinds of scenarios, different people played in different skits, and different races together. I was fascinated and hooked immediately. I had already masturbated a few times but when I became aware that it was coming to an end, I couldn't resist. I checked to see if she was still up at the head of the bed where she couldn't see me and I masturbated again.

Just like I promised, I put the tape back exactly where it was. That night when we went to bed I slept on the floor again. I waited until I thought for sure that she was sleeping and I masturbated a few more times. It's like my brain was a camera and I had cataloged all my favorite parts to my memory. I replayed them repeatedly.

When I woke up the next morning I felt very sleazy and nasty about what I'd done. I needed a bath, but I also wanted to get out of there. I called home, but nobody felt like picking me up. It wasn't that far, I only had to cross two highways, so I walked home from her apartment.

When I got there I immediately went to take a bath. I felt so dirty but even the bath couldn't wash me clean on the inside. Mom asked how my weekend went and I just told her that I never wanted to go over there again. When she asked me why I just told her because the girl's mom wasn't there the entire weekend, which was true. All she said was "huh" and went on about the rest of her Sunday.

I knew that watching things like that was bad, but I couldn't say that I didn't like it. It was the best thing I'd ever seen or done sexually, hands down.

CHAPTER 29

TRACY

The summer after sixth grade my half-brother Elroy had brought his girlfriend Isabelle's nephew back to Georgia to stay with them. His name was Tracy. We were the same age, but he was one school grade higher. The first time I'd ever seen him he'd winked an eye at me and said, "Hey sexy." I turned around and looked behind me because I thought he was talking to someone else.

Nope, he had been talking to me. We were outside; one of the few times that summer that I didn't have Simeon with me. My mother was off from work. I assumed that he was just a boy who had come to visit family for the summer like some of the other kids in the complex.

He then proceeded to tell me that I was going to be his girlfriend and asked me where I lived. I was excited about this because Tracy was a very cute boy. He was tall, slim, wonderfully straight white teeth, and had extremely dark skin that was as smooth and beautiful as a baby's. He had hair that grew into natural, beautiful curls.

I didn't know this at the time, but I'd gone to school with his younger brothers in Louisiana. I'd never seen hair like theirs. He was never with them back then. He had that same type of hair, but it was cut short because he didn't like it. His would forever be the physique I sought after in a mate. Tracy was my first love.

When I told him where I lived I didn't believe him when he said that he'd just come out of that very apartment. To prove it, he called my nephew Roy over to explain that he was his cousin. We spent the rest of that day holding hands and talking. We had so much in common.

One day Marie had decided to take a bunch of us to a movie theatre to go and see a movie, my first in an actual theatre. Tracy asked if he could go, but she didn't have enough money for him, plus there was no more room in the car. Tracy then told her that he had his own money and he'd also pay for me to go. That changed her mind quickly enough.

She told me that I would have to sit on Tracy's lap and she gave Tracy a very serious look and told him, "No funny business!" Tracy just smiled and assured her that he wouldn't touch me. I had been afraid that I was going to squish him. When we were underway I asked him if I was too heavy and he told me no, that he liked big girls. That statement boggled my mind.

I stayed quiet for the rest of the ride, feeling rather giddy. Not more than five minutes into the drive I felt something hard up against my bottom. When I turned wide eyed to look at Tracy, he just smiled. My eyes got even wider as it kept growing. By the feel of it, Tracy's manhood was bigger than anything I'd ever encountered. When my eyes got even wider at the realization his smile just got bigger until I started smiling too.

My main goal from then on out was to see and touch him. It was very frustrating because whenever he came over there were always my nieces and nephews because my older sisters and brothers were going out. So, there was always someone around and, of course, Roy and Darrell wouldn't go away because they were waiting on him to leave.

It took them a few visits to get the hint that I was interested in only Tracy when they came over. The one time that we were alone at my mom's apartment he would let me touch him through his pants, but he wouldn't let me see, afraid that someone would come back into the living room and catch us. Mainly, he was afraid of my mom catching us. I tried to convince him that she'd never come out of her room but he wouldn't believe me.

The only thing that Tracy wanted to do there was kiss. And he didn't want a peck on the cheek. He wanted tongue and all, the one thing that grossed me out. I'd try it just for him, but as soon as I felt the tip of his tongue against mine I'd pull away disgusted. He would just laugh at me and say I didn't give it a chance, that I had to experience a full kiss before I said I didn't like it.

I was sexually frustrated on a constant basis because I couldn't get what I wanted from him. Once, right before school started, we had all been left at Elroy's house. I had just turned fourteen at the end of July. Daniel and Derrick were supposed to be in charge for a change. Roy had a video gaming system in his room, that's where Daniel and Derrick ended up, along with all the boys. The girls were going between Jewel's room and the living room.

I had been sitting on the sofa when Tracy called me into the master bedroom under some pretense so that no one would be suspicious. When I got there, he closed the door and put his arms around me. Immediately he tried to kiss me, but I told him I didn't want to do that. When he asked me what I wanted to do, I told him I wanted to hunch, pants down.

He agreed and told me to lie on the floor. I laid down and pulled my pants and panties down to mid-thigh, he did the same. I was watching him when he did it and I could not believe my eyes. I didn't get to look and touch like I wanted to because as soon as his pants were down he was on top of me. It didn't matter; I was finally getting something I wanted. This was different than anything I'd ever experienced because he was my boyfriend and I felt like that made it alright.

As we were hunching he kissed me lightly across my lips. Then the next thing I knew he was putting his tongue in my mouth. But this time instead of protesting I let him do it because I didn't want to halt progress on other things that I was enjoying.

At first, I held my tongue still while he explored and swirled his around mine. Okay, it wasn't that bad. So, I tried to imitate what he was doing with his tongue. When I did, a whole new sensation erupted in my body, from my tongue all the way down to where the other part of our bodies touched. It was a feeling that I had never experienced before, it was indescribable.

In the next instant, there was a bang on the door and Elroy was asking who had locked his bedroom door. We both jumped up quickly and I ran to the bathroom. I asked Tracy in a panic what we were going to do. He just told me to close the door and lock it. As I was doing so I saw him walking towards the bedroom door and straightening his clothing.

I pulled my pants down all the way and sat down on the toilet praying that Elroy wouldn't suspect anything. I heard him say, "What are you doing in here? Who's in the bathroom?" I was terrified as I listened to Tracy give him some excuse. "Uh huh, why was the door locked then?" Tracy mumbled something else, but I could tell by Elroy's reply that he didn't believe him.

"Hurry up and come out of there, girl, I have to use the bathroom!" I told him that I was trying as I heard Tracy leaving the room. I couldn't clean up fast enough. I was shocked at how much of a mess I was. I had never seen so much wetness in my private area before and it took me a few minutes to get rid of it. Soon enough, Elroy got tired of waiting and said he was going to the other bathroom.

After that I took a deep breath, exhaled, finished up and left the bathroom. I had to go face the music. When I got out there Tracy was sitting on the sofa, I took the recliner that was the farthest away from him. He whispered that everything was fine, but I couldn't calm my heart from beating so fast.

When Elroy came out of the bathroom he looked at us with a knowing smirk on his face. "Y'all better be careful, you know where that kind of stuff leads, don't ya?" he said then burst into laughter as he walked outside and left. I never got approached about it later so I assumed he never told anyone. We didn't get a chance like that again, though I longed for it every single day.

I spent a good bit of that summer fantasizing about Tracy. So much so that I pretty much left Simeon alone completely. I almost never touched him. My mind was always on Tracy. I didn't see much of him after that. Everyone was preparing for school to start while my mind stayed occupied with lustful thoughts. I knew what they were because my mom talked about it a lot.

She talked about sex outside of marriage, people doing unholy things to each other's bodies, masturbation, and thinking nasty thoughts. All of which, in her estimation, were leading you straight to hell. I was going to hell and I knew it. I couldn't stop myself from thinking the thoughts that I did about Tracy. I had gotten saved but I hadn't changed my life one bit.

I was still hunching with Daniel. Once school started and I got tired of not seeing Tracy I started back molesting Simeon again. I was heading down and I was angry at myself for not being able to control my behavior. I'd fantasize about committing suicide a lot. I felt like it was the only way out. It was the only way that I knew I'd stop for sure.

But that only made me hate God and myself even more. I was too cowardly to go through with it and because of God, I'd go straight to hell. Why would He want to keep someone like me here hurting other people? Why couldn't He grant me a reprieve for doing this? I was making the world a better place. I was sure that the world would agree if you asked.

CHAPTER 30

SEVENTH GRADE

This year was different, better in some ways and worse in others. Better because both Laila and Skye were on the same team as me. I was excited about that. What made it even better is that Laila and I had the same homeroom teacher so we had most of our classes together. Skye had a different homeroom teacher, but we saw her often.

This year we had four teachers, one for each core subject; English, Math, Social Studies, and Science. Skye, Laila, and I were all in the same math class though because somehow, we had been placed in advanced math. I always wondered how I got placed into that class. I don't know whether it was Mrs. Steele or some kind of testing that I don't remember. I loved it though, it was very fun and everything we were learning seemed like totally new material.

Though Mrs. Matthews never substituted for any more of my classes in sixth grade she'd made it a point to speak to me every time she saw me. At first it was weird because she seemed a bit afraid. It made me wonder why she even spoke at all. But as time went on our little brief greetings turned into brief conversations.

Early on in my seventh-grade year she approached me and told me that she would be substituting for one of my elective teachers for two days. She told me that she didn't want an incident like the one we had last year and wanted to know if I could promise that it wouldn't happen. I told her I could never promise what I would or wouldn't do on a day to day basis, it all depended on whether anyone messed with me or not.

So, she asked if I'd like an incentive. When I nodded, she explained that if I was good she would buy me an ice cream at lunch the second day after she substituted. I didn't believe her so I said I wanted my ice cream the day she started substituting and she'd just have to trust me. I wasn't taking any chances. If she didn't give me that ice cream at lunch I was going to raise hell that last day.

The next day I came to class and quietly sat and did the packet of worksheets the teacher had left. All the students in the class were anticipating that I'd do something. Word always travels fast around school and they knew that I was particularly bad with certain teachers and substitutes. When I didn't do anything, someone asked why I was being so quiet.

I looked up at Mrs. Matthews and she nervously smiled at me. I could see that she was hoping that I'd hold up my end of the deal. I turned back to the student who had spoken, put my finger to my lips, shushed him and said that I was trying to do my work. For the rest of the period everyone stayed quiet and we all finished our worksheets a few minutes before the bell rang. She even let us all talk when we were done.

Looking quite satisfied with my behavior she told me that she would see me at lunch and she thanked me for being so well behaved. True to her word, she called me over to the ice cream stand at lunch and bought me an ice cream. She then asked me if I knew that I was a leader. Huh? I was confused by her statement and it probably showed on my face.

She explained that, because I was good, everyone else decided to be also. She said the students had looked to me to set the tone for the class period. She told me that was something to think about and that she appreciated me for keeping my word. The next day I did the same and from then on out we would have small chats in the hallways when I saw her. She seemed genuinely concerned about how I was doing. I never acted out in any of her classes again.

Periodically, I'd talk to Laila on the phone. She still wasn't much of a talker but she'd stay on the phone as long as I wanted to talk. I'd say all kinds of things, as if I was being funny, just to see her reaction to it. One of these things was that I was going to invite myself to sleep over at her house since she never asked. She just laughed and said that was a good idea, I should come over.

I was always of the mindset that people really didn't want me bothering them or coming over to their homes because that's what Mom always said. Whenever any of us asked to sleep over at someone's house she always said, "Don't nobody want y'all at they house bothering them!" And that was the end of the story as far as she was concerned.

I was surprised that she'd let me go to Mrs. Steele's and Ashley's house last year. I would never go by Ashley's ever again though. I think she liked me more than a friend and I didn't want to have to put up with that just to play video games, eat junk food all day, and watch pornos. It wasn't worth it to me.

So, I asked my mom if I could sleep over at Laila's, but she told me no. She had gone back to her usual saying, that they didn't want me over there. When I told Laila this she told me that it wasn't true. That she really wanted me to come over. What needs to be understood about Laila though is that even if she really wants something the inflection in her voice never changes. So, you'd never know whether she meant it or not, there wasn't much enthusiasm in how she came across.

So, we talked about it for a few weeks. I kept asking Mom and she kept giving the same response. Then one Friday Laila said that her mom wanted to speak with my mother. When I put her on the phone, Mom went into her usual proper speaking voice, it was always funny to me, and it never ceased to make me laugh.

Mom said yes a few times and said that she didn't mind. I was dying to know what they were saying. Then she handed the phone back to me and Laila asked where I lived. I told her to come the same way she would to the elementary school, but to take the street that goes behind it and that we lived in building B. She said okay and that they were on their way and hung up the phone.

I stood there stunned for a moment then I asked Mom what that was all about. She just told me to pack a bag because I was going to sleep over at Laila's house until Sunday. I was so excited that I shouted yes and ran to my room. I packed my bag, but as I was packing I was worrying.

I was ashamed of where we lived and that our furniture didn't match. I wondered what Ms. Michelle would think about our place. I was sure that theirs was much nicer because Laila was always dressed nicely. I thought that maybe Ms. Michelle wouldn't like me so much or wouldn't want me to be Laila's friend because we were poor. I didn't want them to come inside. I didn't want them to see how we lived. The apartment was clean because mom had been home that day, but still, I wished that it looked nicer.

When they came, they didn't stay long. They just stood right inside the door. Ms. Michelle introduced herself to my mom and they spoke briefly. Mom was always shy around strangers so she didn't say much. I looked at Ms. Michelle's face to gauge what she thought of the place, but she just seemed nice and cheerful. I hadn't seen her since fifth grade, but she still seemed very nice.

On our way out she asked me how I'd been and gave me a side hug on the way to the car. I absolutely loved Ms. Michelle. I jokingly told her that I had been wondering when she was going to come and adopt me, it felt like I had been waiting forever. She just laughed and laughed and told me that I was silly.

Laila and I had a great weekend. We talked, played games, and watched TV all weekend. We even called Skye and talked with her for a while. She was sad because she couldn't come over.

Laila had tried to get me to sleep in her bed and I'd told her no. We argued over this for a while the first night. She told me that if I didn't want to sleep with her she would sleep on the floor. When I still said no she told me that it wasn't polite to let guests sleep on the floor. I repeatedly told her that I was fine on the floor. The first night we both slept on the floor. The second night she tried to get me to sleep in the bed again, but I still slept on the floor. She slept in the bed.

She just didn't understand. I thought that Laila was perfect, in a good way. To me, she was clean and I was dirty. Laila seemed like all innocence and flowers and I was just bad and dirty and disgusting on the inside. I felt like if I slept beside her either my dirtiness would rub off on her or she would see me as filthy and unclean if she got close enough.

When Sunday afternoon came around Ms. Michelle asked me if I was ready to go home and I flat out told her no. She looked concerned by my response and she left the room for a while. She came back an hour or so later and asked the same question and I told her no again. I said that she should just adopt me and I could just stay there.

She gave me a sad smile, sat on Laila's bed, and sent Laila away to do something. When she told me to come and sit next to her on the bed I got nervous. She asked me why I didn't want to go home and I told her that I didn't like it there. When she asked me why I said that I just don't, that I liked being over by her house and I wished that I didn't have to go home.

She told me that I could stay for two more hours but then she'd have to take me home because she was sure that my mother would miss me. I told her that my mother never missed me, she could keep me for a week and Mom wouldn't even call and ask about me. She told me she didn't believe that. I told her she could believe what she wanted to, that I knew the truth, and if she stuck around long enough she would too.

After she left the room Laila came back in. I didn't feel like playing much, so we just sat and talked quietly. She asked me what was wrong and I just reiterated that I didn't want to go back home. She tried her best to get me back into a good mood, but nobody could make home sound good to me. Home was the worst place ever. Nobody seemed to understand that because they had good homes.

When the time came, I got dropped off. The only thing that made me feel any better was that Ms. Michelle said that I was welcome to come back and sleep over again any time. After that I slept over at Laila's house a lot. At first it was a struggle to convince my mom that they wanted me over. Either Laila or Ms. Michelle would have to ask for my mom to believe it.

After a while Mom just let me go when I wanted to. All I would have to do was ask Laila or Ms. Michelle, but I always told Mom where I was going. I never asked her. Ms. Michelle would always check with me to see if I had asked Mom if I could go because, when they came I'd already be outside waiting. I just told her the truth, no I hadn't asked, but I did tell her where I was going. I think she found it odd that a seventh grader could tell her mother she was leaving and just go.

That was my escape, I'd always leave before anyone left Simeon with me on Fridays and I wouldn't come back until Sunday. I spent more days over if we got days off from school. Ms. Michelle would always make me call my mother if we had a phone. She'd stand there and listen in astonishment because I would just tell my mother I was staying extra days.

She would then ask if I was sure that was my mother. After she'd done this a few times I started giving her the phone before or after I spoke with Mom just so she could see I wasn't making it up. I saw clearly through her reactions that she would never just let her children go where they pleased for however long they decided. It was because she loved her children, I was under the impression that my mom didn't love me.

Eventually, Skye slept over on the same weekends that I did and their moms started calling us the three musketeers. I felt more like the third wheel though because I hadn't known that Ms. Michelle and Ms. Elaine were like best friends. That meant that Skye and Laila hung out more together than I did with either one of them. When I would be there they'd always be laughing after Skye would say or do one little thing and, when I'd ask what they were laughing about, Skye would just say it was an inside joke and keep laughing.

It made me feel like I wasn't in the inside, even though their moms thought so. I couldn't understand why she didn't just tell me so that I could laugh too. That always made me feel insecure and I started to believe that she was using certain words and phrases to tease me without my knowing. I thought that they were both laughing at me.

I'd always ask Laila about it over the phone during the week or on weekends when Skye wasn't there and she'd explain the whole thing to me. But by the next time Skye came over they'd have something else private to laugh about. Sometimes Skye would also talk over me when I was trying to say something. So, I was mostly quiet when Skye was there unless she was talking directly to me.

I would still come over even if I knew she'd be there though because it was still better than being at home. Plus, Laila would always fall asleep around nine at night and once she was asleep you could not wake her up. I always got along great with Skye when Laila wasn't around. I didn't feel like I had to compete with Skye then. We'd laugh and talk just as much as she would with Laila. I just couldn't understand why it was different when all three of us got together.

I was also jealous because, even though Skye and I were the same height, she and Laila were closer in size. They dressed alike a lot and I'd always have on baggy clothing. They had a lot more in common. The only times that I enjoyed was when they would try to get me to be more feminine in certain ways. I'd refuse to comply.

I remember once when they'd both sat on me in an attempt to hold me down and put make-up on me and paint my nails. I did a push-up with them both on my back and they screamed, got scared, and got off before I could get all the way up. I just laughed and laughed because they thought they'd come up with a foolproof plan to subdue me.

This year was also the worst because it was the year I got picked on more than any other year in school. By then I thought that I was extremely ugly, fat, and that I looked like a man. All the boys at school thought so too. That's what they teased me about most times because I was too muscular and looked like a man. It's what got me into major trouble most days.

Laila had talked me into wearing a dress for picture day. So, I'd worn a jumper dress that had cow prints at the top where the belted parts were. After lunch, I was standing in the line to leave the cafeteria and a group of boys were whispering at a table near the exit line. I heard one of them say something about a fat cow and when I looked at him they all giggled.

It was Skye's boyfriend talking. When I told him I'd heard what he said he shouted, "What's a boy doing wearing girl's clothes?" All his friends burst into laughter. This was the first time I'd worn a dress to school since kindergarten and he'd just made me the most uncomfortable I'd ever been at school.

I couldn't do my usual because I was afraid to fight him in a dress. So, I told him that if he didn't shut his mouth I'd beat him up. I was thinking that the threat would make him scared. It usually did, by now, all I had to do was threaten people to get them to leave me alone.

This time though, he decided to show off in front of his friends and tell me that I'd have to catch him first. Then he said that since I was so fat that would never happen. I just said, "Okay, we'll see." But I was steaming mad and Laila could tell because she kept rubbing my back and saying that it was okay, they were just being stupid boys.

I shoved her hand away because I knew if she kept at it I would start crying in front of everyone. That would've been the ultimate downfall for me, I never cried at school or in front of my friends. I was still angry when I called her after school. I just knew in my mind that Skye had been talking bad about me to her boyfriend. Laila kept telling me that Skye wouldn't do that and that I should call Skye.

When I did, she told me that she would never talk about me behind my back. She said that we were friends and I should never think she'd say bad things about me. When I told her that I was going to beat her boyfriend up, she begged me not to. She said that if I fought him I might mess up his face and he was too cute for me to do that.

I thought that it would be good for him if I did. But she was adamant about me not beating him up so I devised another plan. I snuck up behind him every chance I got and I would breathe on the back of his neck or whisper that I thought he said I'd never catch him. He'd immediately scream like a girl and run. He was the laughingstock of seventh grade. I was having the time of my life teasing him. I loved the fear I could put into him just by breathing.

For days, I tortured him by sneaking up on him. I started telling him that one of these days I was just going to walk up and beat him down. I teased him so bad at lunch that he stopped going altogether. A few days after that happened I got called to the seventh-grade administrator's office.

When I arrived, there sat Skye's boyfriend, looking quite fearful of me. I smiled at him menacingly and he shrank down into his seat. The administrator asked me to have a seat. When I did, we were side by side sitting across from her. She said that for the past few days she'd gone to the main office to find him sitting in there because he refused to eat in the cafeteria. When she asked him why he told her it was because I was going to beat him up.

She turned to me and asked me to assure him that a nice girl like me wouldn't do such a thing. I looked her in the eye and told her I wasn't so nice. Then I turned to him and said that sooner or later he was going to get it. He looked to her immediately afraid, hands gesturing toward me and saying, "You see what I mean?"

With a very stern expression she asked if I was really going to threaten him in front of her. Asking if I knew how much trouble I could get into by taking this route, telling me that she could write me up that instant and send me to In School Suspension or worse. I told her that I didn't care what she did, that if I decided that I was going to beat someone up,

I'd do it regardless of the consequences.

Bewildered, and clearly at a loss for words, she sat back for a moment thinking. Then she asked why it was that I wanted to fight him. I told her everything that had transpired on picture day, even the fact that I never wore dresses to school. By the end of it, I had done the very thing I said I'd never do at school, I was in tears. When she turned back to him he had shrunken further down into his seat. He had not told her that part of the story.

She told him in a very serious tone that what he had done was unacceptable and asked if he had anything to say for himself. He said that he hadn't started the teasing, that it was his friends who had started it all and then looked to him in anticipation of what he would say. He said that he really had nothing bad to say about me, that I was his girlfriend's best friend, but he thought his friends would tease him if he said so. That's when he'd made the comments he did and those were the ones that I heard. When I'd responded to him he couldn't back down or else his friends would think he was a punk.

By this time, he was also crying and looking rather ashamed of himself. I didn't know whether it was real or if he was faking it so that she wouldn't be so angry at him. She told him to look at the mess he'd started by falling into peer pressure. That all we had done was to hurt each other for no reason at all. She told us to face each other, talk it out, and apologize. We did as she asked and he seemed sincere about it.

She let him go, but made me stay behind to talk with her. Ever since seventh grade had started I'd been in her office or standing outside of it at least once a week. One teacher or another would send me to her for my behavior. Even though my grades were okay I'd push past the envelope often, mostly in the extracurricular classes.

I'd always love sitting outside her office when she wasn't there. Students would pass by and ask what I'd done this time and I'd proudly tell them whatever it was and they'd tell me I was so bad, even upperclassmen knew who I was and I thought that was very cool.

She had a talk with me about my behavior in general. She wanted to know why I took so much pride in getting in trouble. She asked if I needed to talk to her about some other things that were bothering me. As always, there was no way in my mind that I thought I could tell her what was really wrong. There was no way she would understand any of what was happening to me or what I was doing. Inside, I was a really bad person. What I did at school just couldn't compare. There was no way I could get her to understand.

So, I told her that I didn't have anything to say. She then pointed out that she had a candy jar on her shelf that was full of candy. And that every week that I had good behavior I could come up to the office between classes on Fridays and get a piece. I understood what she was trying to do, but I had gotten much more at times for just being good for a day or two. I looked at this as a joke.

I told her I'd try just to appease her so that she would let me leave. As time went on I may have gotten a piece of candy two or three times, but it wasn't from any effort of mine to stay out of trouble. Most times she would have to remind me to come and get some candy because I'd really paid no mind to what she had said and didn't realize that I had gone a week without getting in trouble.

Sometimes I'd get away with things though. Like this one time when I'd gotten on the bus. I always had a particular seat I liked to sit in. Well, one day a sixth grader named Antwoine was sitting there. When I told him that he was sitting in my seat he said, "So!" and he continued to sit there. I just said fine and decided to sit with him.

When I put my book bag down, he shoved it onto the floor. I told him that I was going to be nice to him and ignore that, but that I was going to sit in my seat whether he was in it or not. When I tried to sit my bag down again he punched me in my chest. Immediately, I snapped and began punching him in his face, beating him down into the seat.

When he tried to wedge his feet in between us to kick me away I grabbed the collar of his shirt and threw him into the seat across from where we were. Another kid punched him a few times while I changed positions to kick him. I kicked him until his body lodged between the seats towards the floor.

By then the bus driver had made her way back to where we were and students had started to grab me and pull me away from him. At that moment, my anger seemed like it increased tenfold and I went charging for him again. No one was going to force me to stop and since I was already in trouble I might as well get every lick in that I possibly could.

But people kept grabbing my arms every time I reared back to punch him and I could no longer reach him like I wanted to, stuffed between the seats. So, with one arm I grabbed a hold to his neck and pulled him up as I fought to get my other arm free. When I did so I wrapped both hands around his neck and started to squeeze.

Everyone was screaming and yelling, pushing and shoving, and Antwoine was grasping at my hands with no real effect. I could hear the bus driver, she was right there in my ear telling me to let go of him. She seemed eerily calm while doing so. But I couldn't let him go, my anger wouldn't let me. If I was going to get in trouble it was going to be for something, I was going to finish this, once and for all.

People were going to stop picking at me. I was tired, I was tired of absolutely everything and I wanted to make a real impact. Maybe if I taught him a lesson, everyone would leave me alone. I wanted them to put me away. I was ready to go. I was enraged at everything in my life. But even as I was thinking all of this, I had doubts, a small part of me wanted to stop. A part that said there was no turning back from this.

But the bigger part of me said that I was already in trouble so, what was the point in stopping now? Then there was the bus driver, still there amongst all the chaos, speaking to me as calmly and as peacefully as if there was no pandemonium. It was very strange that I could hear her over everything else, as if her voice dwelled on the inside of me. She said, "If you let him go, I won't write you up." And in that instant, I let him go.

When I did, everyone fell silent. I looked to see those closest to me looking at me wide eyed and in terror. That's when I realized what I could have done. Some of those further back were smiling, enjoying the drama of it all, and reveling in it. I sat down shaking, all the rage dissipating quickly now.

I stared out the window blankly as I heard the bus driver leading Antwoine to the front. When I did glance at them, she was pulling him by his ear. He was feeling well enough to be angrily voicing his opinion that she should have written me up. They continued to the front as she told him to shut up and that she saw him throw the first punch. In her estimation, he was lucky that I hadn't killed him.

We lived in a predominantly black apartment complex. And Mrs. Jackson, who was also black, had always been our bus driver. No one else wanted our route and even though she was older, she was the only driver who would take our route. She was also the only one who seemed to handle it well, nothing ever shook her.

My brother Matthew, who was in sixth grade with Antwoine, was not aware of who had been fighting until we pulled up to the high school and the other students told Daniel as soon as he got on the bus. Matthew never liked to get involved in anything that had drama written all over it. He had never even moved from the front seat during the fight. That's where Matthew stayed, in the front right side seat of every bus we ever rode, always talking to the bus driver.

There was excitement on the bus now, everyone was anticipating what was going to happen when Antwoine's older brother got on the bus. I was dreading it because Dre was a really bad boy. He was the reason why the pizza men from Domino's, Pizza Hut, and Papa John's wouldn't deliver in our apartment complex. He had beaten up the delivery men and taken all the cash they had on them. The only reason I knew that is because he was friends with my brothers and they had told me. The cops never found out who it was.

It didn't matter that they were friends though. Dre would fight at the drop of a hat for any reason. I was worried because Derrick had not come to the bus yet. With just Daniel who couldn't fight and Matthew who probably wouldn't, I was going to be in real big trouble. I still felt somewhat comforted that they were there, I just didn't feel confident. Dre could do a lot of damage when he was angry, that made me scared.

By the time Daniel had reached my seat he had gotten an ear full. He asked me what was going on. I pulled him down into my seat and, instead of explaining the fight, I was warning him of the fight to come. I didn't have time for what had transpired, I wanted to make sure we were ready and Dre didn't take us by surprise. So, Daniel decided to sit in my seat. He sat next to the aisle just in case Dre got crazy.

I was watching through the window, heart beating out of my chest as Dre approached the line to board the bus. I was so relieved to see Derrick walk up behind him. As soon as they stepped on, both got the news at the same time. Antwoine was slumped over in his seat trying to avoid his brother because he had gotten beaten up by a girl. While Dre was angrily asking his brother what happened, Derrick was leaning over Matthew's seat talking to him. I was hoping that he knew enough to warn him of what was about to happen.

I watched as Dre's muscles bunched bigger and his body grew tense. He pushed Antwoine and asked him something that he seemed like he did not want to tell. Then, reluctantly, Antwoine turned around and pointed in my direction.

Immediately, Dre came stomping towards the back of the bus, fists balled at his sides. And just as fast both Derrick and Matthew followed while Daniel rose to stand in front of me. I didn't know how this would end, but in that moment, I was so glad to be riding the same bus as my brothers and proud that they would stand up for me. That's something they didn't do most of the time.

When he stopped in front of Daniel, Dre took off his shirt and threw it to the floor in anger. The high school girls in the back loudly expressed their pleasure as his muscles swelled. He told Daniel to move out of his way. Daniel told him no while Derrick let his presence be known by saying Daniel wasn't moving anywhere unless it was to let him pick up his shirt and go sit down somewhere other than next to me. Matthew followed that up with a loud, "Yeah!"

What should have made a normal person back down made Dre angrier. He asked if we were all going to jump him now like I had jumped his brother. He said that I was too big to be fighting his little brother and he was going to teach me a lesson. I told him that his brother threw the first punch and he said it didn't matter, that no one beats up his little brother.

The high school girls from the back walked up touching him on his chest and arms, telling him that he shouldn't start a fight where he'll get in trouble. They told him he should wait until after we get off the bus. They were saying all this while touching and caressing his chest, arms, and back. Visibly distracted, Dre let them pull him the rest of the way to the back of the bus.

Mrs. Jackson had been talking to another bus driver out the window the entire time. When she saw Dre, she yelled for him to put his shirt back on, which he did after it was handed back to him. The bus was electrified with excitement as we rode home from school that day. When we got off the bus everyone just stood around, which made Mrs. Jackson sit there and wait. She was trying to make sure nothing went on so everyone started walking towards the apartment complex and she pulled off.

As soon as she did, Dre came after me but all my brothers and their friends pushed him back and held him down. They were trying to reason with him and tell him that it was his brother's fault. People were telling him that he should know how obnoxious his brother can be. Then someone mentioned that another boy had even punched Antwoine a few times during the fight.

When Dre heard this, he said fine and visibly calmed down. But when they let him go he went after the other boy and beat him up. My brothers and I walked home while Dre followed us. He was yelling that he would find me and beat me up when no one was around. Reagan came around the corner of our building. She was back in Georgia now that she had dropped out of LSU.

I had spent only two years in school with Reagan. She had been in fourth and fifth grade and I was in Kindergarten both times. During that time, no one had ever picked on me because if they had, everyone knew that she was going to get them. Ever since she'd left, I had to fight for myself because my brothers were always too scared to do anything up until now.

Even though Dre was bigger, that didn't intimidate Reagan one bit. She walked up to him, put her finger in his face and gave him the business. By the time she was finished fussing, he looked very afraid. From then on out he never spoke one word to me. I never understood how he could be so afraid of one person when he'd had no problem harassing and trying to fight four people at once.

My unspoken wish was granted when I went back to school the next day. Kids from other buses in the bus lane had seen me fighting through the windows. On top of that, those from my bus were telling everyone, saying that I'd almost choked a boy to death. Everyone either gave me a wide berth or they became good friends with me. From then on out I didn't have trouble with kids teasing me at school anymore.

Of course, all this talk got me pulled into the administrator's office, but I played dumb. Surprisingly, so did Antwoine. Mrs. Jackson had told him that if she wrote me up he would have to get in trouble too because he started the fight. Eventually, even Antwoine and I became friends. He was the one who always professed the loudest that people shouldn't mess with me. They'd get back far worse than what they dished out.

As for the administrator, she thought that she was the reason why I calmed down in school. She was under the impression that her talk and candy was what swayed me to better behavior in school. I told her no different. Even though it wasn't much, I still enjoyed getting a little piece of candy once a week. I let her believe what she wanted.

CHAPTER 31

THE SUBSTITUTE DRIVER

Mrs. Jackson rarely missed a day driving her school bus, but when she did I always felt sorry for the substitute. Everyone on our bus knew that all the other bus drivers dreaded our route. We were one of the worst bus routes a driver could have, if not the worst. But this day was different from all the others. This substitute driver had a secret weapon, something we had never experienced before. This driver had a stereo system installed in her nice, new bus.

First of all, to see a brand-new bus come to pick us up was unheard of. When she pulled up, everyone stood still, staring. We all thought we were going to be riding in style that day! Matthew was excited as well because he loved all things automotive and couldn't wait to talk with the bus driver about all the new features on her bus.

When the doors opened, we all fought to be one of the first to get on the bus. Our excitement doubled once we boarded because she had music playing through speakers that sat over the windows in intervals that spanned the length of the bus. The music wasn't exactly to our taste, but to my surprise, she changed it to our favorite R&B and Hip-Hop station. I thought for sure they were going to play something she would disapprove of and she'd change the station.

Surprisingly, they did not. What they did play though, was R. Kelly's new song "I Believe I Can Fly". Every single student on the bus loved that song. And as we rode the bus to school, everyone that I could see was singing the song. And it was like nothing else we'd ever done. Usually, kids would over sing or sing a song in a silly way to make others laugh. It was like everyone was singing the song from their hearts that day.

Everybody in my neighborhood who rode this bus, no matter the age, had experienced something in our young lives that had already broken our hearts. Everyone knew how it felt to break down, feel like giving up, or had already given up. This song personally meant something to all of us. And as we sang in unison, without flaw, I watched everything and everyone.

I saw sadness and tears come to the eyes of some of my fellow students. I saw far away looks from those who had lived a better life than this. I saw the scenery pass by in muted, slow motion, as if it were witnessing the beauty of our pain and sorrow instead of us witnessing the beauty of nature. And as hope arose in the song, I could hear the desperation of hope coming from the devastation of our lives in our voices. All of us praying that one day we would see better days.

All of these things I witnessed, but the most

compelling was the eyes of this bus driver. I don't think that her soul was prepared to hear such an outcry. In all her years, I'm sure she'd heard many stories about this route, and I am quite certain by the look on her face that this was the very last thing she'd expected.

I saw tears form in her eyes as they changed from the mundane to a look of amazement. I witnessed the way that she swallowed and fought back the tears as she drove. I could see that she was truly affected by our voices.

I did not want this time to end. If I could have been suspended there, I would have. Because, life as I had known it had very few happy times. This moment was full of hopes and dreams and even change. But my life experiences had taught me that change wasn't always for the better. If I could keep this moment of hope, if I could hold onto this feeling that I could rise above all that has me trapped, I could truly live my life to the finish.

And as we pulled into the bus lane, the song ended, and for moments after there was nothing but silence. The bus driver stood and turned to face us, eyes dried but still emotion filled.

And then she spoke, "You guys were awesome! I've never heard a group of kids sing like that before. Are you all in a choir together or something?" Someone shouted back, "Are you for real, lady? A choir!" Almost the entire bus laughed as the bell rang and she opened the door to let us off. The moment was gone.

I was the last to get off the bus. Her face still expressed disbelief as she watched each student step down and go about their day as if what just happened did not occur. When I approached, we made eye contact and I just smiled back at her. Everyone else had pretended like it wasn't a big deal and she was such a lame for even commenting on it, but I knew better.

As I passed her to get off the bus she sighed and raised both hands in the air, head shaking. She was taken aback still at what she had just heard and the response she had gotten from her praise. In our neighborhood, kids did amazing things all the time. We all had talents and gifts. What she couldn't fathom is that in our home lives, some of us weren't encouraged or complimented on these things. She had gotten a dose of what we had been raised with, ridicule and laughter.

CHAPTER 32

GOING BACKWARDS

Daniel continued to beg me about letting him "stick it in". During my seventh-grade year, he was the worst thing I had to deal with at home. Sometimes we would even argue for a while before we ever hunched. He'd sit there and wait to see if I would agree and I'd be waiting for him to give up on the notion. It was always nerve racking to me that he seemed so obsessed with this and that he couldn't understand how gross I thought it was. I kept trying to think of a way to make him understand.

One day I came up with what I thought was a brilliant idea. If I couldn't get him to change his mind I thought maybe I could go back to hunching with Matthew or Derrick. I didn't think that they would be as bad as Daniel and I could just stop doing things with him altogether. First though, I'd have to ask one of them.

Because Matthew was younger I was less afraid to ask him. It still didn't take away the nervousness, but because he was younger he seemed like less of a threat than Derrick. So, after committing to this plan, all I had left to do was find a time to broach the subject with him.

I waited for a week or so until one day we were finally alone watching television. Everyone else was either outside or gone. It took me a while to get up the nerve to say anything at first. I mulled through a few scenarios until I found something to say that would seem non-threatening. Then I asked, "Matthew, do you remember when we were little and we used to do things together?"

He asked, "What do you mean?" I explained to him about how we used to play with each other in private after Rachel stopped making us touch each other. He said, "Yeah, what about it?" Then I asked him if he would like to do it again now. He told me no, but it didn't sound all that convincing to me so I asked if he was sure he didn't want to.

He asked me why I wanted to start something like that back up. I just told him that I missed doing it. I didn't want to tell him the real reason because, if he decided to tell on me, that would be giving him more info to tell about. I asked him if he missed doing it and he told me that in some ways he did, but that he wished he could do that with a girl he liked, not his sister.

I told him that I completely understood and that I felt the same way, but nobody that I wanted to do that with would be willing to. Matthew and I were in the same boat in that respect, we'd have a crush on someone, but they'd never notice. If they did they'd make it a point to avoid us, they were more embarrassed by us than flattered. It always happened that way.

So, I set about convincing him to hunch with me. He

didn't want to do it, I knew that. But I kept begging him because I knew he would do it anyway, just to shut me up and stop me from bothering him. When he finally gave in I got on top of him and hunched him until I finished. It was a lot different with him and I had to keep repositioning myself. Matthew was only thirteen and hadn't reached the puberty level that Daniel had. It took longer than it usually would because of this.

When I was finished Matthew immediately burst into tears and, crying loudly, he ran to his room and shut the door. I didn't expect that to happen, but when it did I knew exactly why. I knew how he felt. I knew how ashamed, powerless, and dirty he felt. As I went into the bathroom to wipe off, I cried too.

I knew that all Matthew wanted was for a girl to like him. He didn't want what I had coerced him into doing. I felt just as dirty as I did when I touched Simeon. Even more so because I knew how much he had hated what just happened. I hated myself for being so blind not to see that this was something he really didn't want. And worst of all, I couldn't take it back.

Matthew didn't come out of the room again that day until he was sure someone else was there besides me. I spent the rest of that day wishing I'd never hurt him, wishing I had never asked such a thing of him. For a while I steered clear of Matthew and I never asked him about it again. True to his character, Matthew just pretended like nothing ever happened and he never spoke of it or how he felt about it.

Meanwhile, I was still faced with Daniel and his begging. I continued to say no, I would always say no to him. It was just something that I couldn't give. Even though by now the hunching was mutual I always felt deep down that Daniel had taken something from me, long ago, before I ever had a choice. This time, I had a choice, and I would never give him any more than I already had.

Eventually, his pleading started to wear on me again. When it did I started thinking of Derrick. I just didn't want things to end like they had with Matthew. I thought the simple solution to this was to leave Derrick alone if he said no. After that conclusion, I waited for the right time.

It took me a long time to get up the nerve to ask Derrick though. There were more than a few times that we were alone, but I was just too nervous and scared to ask him. I had more respect for him because he was the one that had decided to stop and he'd told me to tell on Daniel. The telling never ended well and in thinking that I got an idea. I would use that in my defense when I asked him.

Still it took some time before I got up the nerve to say something. I started out the same as before. Asking him if he remembered and then inquiring if he would like to do it again. He seemed a bit puzzled at the conversation and asked if I knew that this was wrong. I told him that I did, but that Daniel and I still do it. He was surprised to hear that information.

I told him not to look so surprised because every time I

told, I got a whipping for telling. He told me sadly that he remembered that, but that Dad wasn't around anymore. Then I told him about the times that I had told Mom and her reaction. She never did anything about it and he knew this.

So, then he asked me why I was asking him if I had already told so many times. That if I kept telling, obviously, I didn't want to do it. I told him that I did like it, but I didn't like that Daniel kept asking me to have sex with him. I told him that I didn't want to do that with Daniel. I knew Derrick was interested when he asked, "How do I know that you won't tell on me?"

I told him because he was different and that I always liked hunching with him, that I never liked it as much with Daniel. He thought for a minute and then said, "Well, what if I don't want that?" When I asked what he wanted he said that he was older now and boys his age, sixteen, wanted to have sex. He said that if I couldn't give him that then he didn't want to do anything because he could go and hunch any girl. I knew this to be true because all the girls liked Derrick.

Deep down inside I hated Daniel for asking, but I didn't hate Derrick. He had a take it or leave it attitude about it. It made me feel like he was offering something that was good and that if I said no I'd be missing out on a great opportunity. In the end, I just felt like it was better than letting Daniel have at it so, I told him that I would do it.

He asked me if I was sure I wanted to do this. Because he even thought enough to ask me, it made me even more secure in my decision. My thoughts were that Derrick was very thoughtful and considerate and I'd rather do something like this with him than Daniel any day. I'd let Derrick usher me into this new part of my life and leave Daniel far behind.

I was fourteen and by this point boys had already been asking and hinting that they wanted to have sex with me. They never wanted me to be their girlfriend, but they would definitely have sex with me. As one boy once told me, "Pussy don't have no face." Basically, I was ugly, but my vagina would always be desirable.

I was used to comments like these and they were the reason why I didn't want to give this gift away to someone who didn't care about me. I felt like Derrick cared so I would give my virginity to him and then I'd be free to have sex when I wanted to and not have to feel like I was giving something precious up to a jackass.

With my plans set I let him coach me on what to do. I took off my pants and my panties and laid on the dining room floor with my legs open. He was very nice in all his instruction, telling me what to expect, that it might hurt a little. At least that's what he had heard. He was doing all of this while removing his clothes. There were a lot of reasons why girls would like him more by the look of him. His body looked more mature in a lot of ways.

He came down on top of me, positioned himself between my legs, and asked if I was sure that I was ready for this. I told him yes and he waited a second then tried to push forward. It hurt immediately, "Ouch!" I said in a sharp whisper. He backed away and said, "I told you it would hurt. You just have to hold still and let me do it."

When I nodded, he asked if I was ready to try again. I said yes and he came forward once more. I had the same reaction as before and scooted up a little to avoid him. Frustration began to show on his face and he just sat looking off to the side for a minute. I asked him why we couldn't just hunch and he said that he'd told me he wasn't going to do that. He meant it.

He tried to talk me into it one more time, but when I did the same thing for the third time he just said, "Forget it." He didn't say it in anger but I saw the disappointment on his face. He got up and told me to forget that this ever happened. When I told him that I was sorry, he said that it wasn't my fault, got dressed, and left.

I had thought that I was ready, but I wasn't. From then on out Derrick was nice to me still. He always was. But we never spoke about what happened that day. I used to wish that I could've done it, especially when it came time to hunch with Daniel. I would want to stop it all together and sometimes I would be able to for a few weeks but then the urge always came back. I would always end up right back where I was, wishing that I wasn't.

After a while of dealing with the arguments with him I decided to tell my mom again. By then I felt like it wasn't really all his fault that we were doing this, but I'd go back to thinking that he was the one who started it all in the first place, so I was justified in telling on him.

Mom and I had the same conversation we always had. She wanted to know how he was messing with me and I'd repeat the same thing, "in a nasty way." I couldn't understand why she needed to know details. I still felt like, had I been the mom, I wouldn't have had to ask for details to catch on to the fact that my son was touching my daughter inappropriately.

The only difference this time is that I thought we were alone in the apartment, but we weren't. As I was trying to explain to her, Charlie was in another room listening. He didn't stay in there for long though. It took him no time to understand what my mother didn't seem to grasp.

He burst into the living room so violently that my father flashed before my eyes. I had to do a double take while my heart pounded in overtime. He yelled, "Who are we talking about?" When I squeaked out that it was Daniel, he immediately left the apartment saying, "Yeah? Well, I'm gon fix him real good today!"

I had not wanted to tell him who it was, but I also didn't want his anger to turn towards me for not telling. I worried badly for Daniel. I knew for sure that Charlie was going to do him bodily harm and I didn't think that Daniel deserved that sort of punishment. I just wanted it all to stop, I didn't want him to get hurt in the process. Still, I just sat there on the sofa scared, waiting.

Minutes later he came bursting back through the door almost literally dragging Daniel behind him. He then lifted him to his feet by his neck and shoved him into the room.

They were quickly followed by Matthew and Derrick who were curious to see what was going on.

Charlie pointed a finger at me and got within an inch of Daniels face, "You been touching on this girl? Huh? Answer me!" he yelled. Daniel didn't say anything. He just stood there with tears rolling down his face, avoiding eye contact with Charlie. He seemed afraid to answer, but at the same time anger exuded from him.

After this, I knew I would not want to have to explain why I told on him. Every time we'd start back up there was always that conversation, but he never came at me angrily. Before we'd start anything he'd always want to know why, but judging by the anger I saw, that conversation wouldn't go well at all. It was almost like hatred was pouring out of him, though he never looked my way, I could feel and see it.

Charlie grabbed him by his jaw and slammed him against the wall. Mom came forward and warned Charlie that he was being too rough. He ignored Mom and roared at Daniel, "You want somebody to touch on? Huh? You want somebody to touch you?" When he said that last part he roughly grabbed Daniel's genitals and shook them.

Then he jabbed his finger hard into Daniel's chest repeatedly as he spoke. "The next time you want somebody to play with, you come to me. I better not ever hear about you touching this girl again. Momma won't be able to save you then. It's gon be me and you!"

Daniel just stood there glaring at him, shaking in what

seemed like a barely controlled rage, tears rolling down his face. He did not speak a word. I thought for sure that Charlie was going to lay into him until he gave verbal confirmation that he understood.

They stood staring at each other as if it were a showdown. Daniel finally took his eyes away to look down. That's when Charlie took him by his shirt and shoved him away shouting, "Get out of my face! I'm tired of looking at your sorry ass!"

Daniel left me alone for weeks after that. Most of the family who stayed in the apartment complex had heard about what had happened and Marie told Mom that I should never be left alone with Daniel. An effort was made for a while, but eventually I started telling Mom that I was fine to stay home, that Daniel wouldn't do anything to me.

In truth, he wouldn't. Daniel rarely ever approached me about hunching. By this time, I initiated the hunching just as much as he did, maybe more. And sure enough, I brought things back around full circle, back to the hunching again. He asked me then why I had told Charlie, but when he asked there was no anger.

I was surprised that he would want to start again and that he asked like he always had. I found that to be strange, but I wasn't going to ask him about it, I just accepted it and explained to him that I hadn't, that Charlie was in another room listening without my knowledge. He asked me not to ever tell Charlie anything again. Out of fear for him, I never did, but something inside of me changed then.

Once when I wanted to take a bath Karen had beat me to it and she was purposely taking her time to annoy me. No one was there except she and I, but I opened the bathroom door and jokingly told her that if she did not get out of the tub I would call Daniel in so that he would see her naked.

When she started to look worried I called out as if he were there. When she began to bathe faster, I laughed. That's how Marie walked up on us. She had heard the entire conversation from the front door to the bathroom and she was angry. She said that it was not something that I should tease about. She looked at me strangely and said, "You clown around as if what you say Daniel did isn't true and that's not something you should joke about." She left it at that and walked away.

But I felt ashamed of what I had just done. I was angry at Karen, but that had given me no right to make her afraid. It also wasn't something I should've laughed at. I had lost my grip on reality and the gravity of the entire situation. Over the years, I had become desensitized and the lines seemed to get grayer as each day passed. Most of all I was worried about what Marie thought of me.

CHAPTER 33

NOBODY KNOWS

As time passed, I became more and more depressed. I started drawing a lot in classes where I didn't like the subject, particularly Science and Social Studies. I did okay with my grades, but that's only because I would see Mrs. Steele from time to time and she would always ask about them. She would ask about my personal life too.

Mrs. Steele never let me have another slumber party, but every now and then she would let me sleep over. I liked those times because she would put me to work on Saturdays. I would cut the grass, pull weeds out of her garden, or dig small trenches around certain spots for her. She always paid me even though I felt like I was getting all the benefits by just being there.

I loved Mrs. Steele so much, more than any other teacher. She was just so kind, even when she didn't realize it, she was kind. When I slept over I'd always wake up early in the morning ready for the day, but I would never get up. I would lay there and wait until she came downstairs into the guest room to come and get me.

When she came in I'd be lying on my stomach

pretending that I was asleep. I did this because she would come and sit on the bed and gently call my name, like I imagined a loving mother would call her child. When I didn't respond, she would rub my back and coax me into waking up. She was always so gentle and I loved that about her. I felt bad about pretending to be asleep, but I was so hungry for the love I felt through her touch that I couldn't bring myself not to pretend.

Sometimes she would do something funny though. I remember once when she called my name and when I didn't answer she sat on me and we both burst into laughter. She said, "Get up, sleepy head." And then she left the room. By age fourteen I was a very sturdy kid and she knew that. At other times when I took too long "waking up" she would tickle my sides. Though I looked very serious most of the time, I was extremely ticklish and she'd use that against me, especially when I was awake.

But, no matter how she "woke me up", it was never in a mean way. I just couldn't understand how nice she could be compared to my mother. Mom wasn't really mean, she was just cold in a way. Instead of waking you up nicely, she would yell and basically scare you awake. If you were sick, she'd buy the medicine, but gripe and fuss about the reason you'd gotten sick in the first place. When all you would want is to be loved and hugged on, Mom would do the total opposite.

With Mrs. Steele and all the other mother figures in my life it was all warmth, always warmth. I could never sit as close to my mother as I did Mrs. Steele. I never even hugged Mom, but it was customary to hug Mrs. Steele or Ms. Michelle. They would be insulted sometimes when I would forget.

Once when Mrs. Steele brought me home, no one was there, but I had a key. She came inside with me and since no one was there I showed her the room I shared with my little sister Karen. When she got ready to go she told me to come and give her a kiss. Immediately I was alarmed because she's never asked for a kiss before. When she saw my expression, she said that it was okay and tried to coerce me into giving her a kiss goodbye on her cheek.

The closer she came to me the more fearful I became. With every step she took, I took one backwards and I began to shake my head. That's when she really saw it, recognized that something was wrong. She asked me if I knew that she would never hurt me. When I didn't answer, she told me that it was okay, I didn't have to give her a kiss.

She then asked for a hug instead, but I was already too freaked out by the thought of kissing her that I just shook my head no. Then she looked at me strangely. Her face showed that she was hurt, but not like I had hurt her. She looked as if she hurt for me. Then she said, "Okay, I'm going to go but we're going to have a talk about this. Okay?" And when I agreed she turned and left.

The next time I stayed after on a Friday to sleep over at her house we had that talk before we even left school. She asked me if someone had ever done something or touched me in an inappropriate way. When I told her no she told me not to lie, that there's only one reason why I would react that way towards her.

I didn't want to lie to her. I had to tell her something. So, we had a long talk leaving school that Friday. We talked a lot. I told her about everything that happened when I was little. I shared about everything that happened to me sexually. I told her all about how my father used to beat me and sometimes make me bleed. I made it seem like I had only been messed with until we moved to Georgia.

I wrapped it all up into a nice, neat little package that ended when we had moved. She asked if I was okay and if I needed to see someone. I said that I was just fine. I told her that I'd learned from all of what happened and that I'd never do something like that to someone else, the sexual abuse or the whippings. And she believed.

But I had lied to her because I couldn't tell her or anybody the things that were happening now. I would get into deep trouble for what I was doing to Simeon and what I participated in with Daniel. Those were things that I couldn't tell anyone. Most of all, I didn't want Mrs. Steele to hate me. No one would ever know because I couldn't bear the hatred of those that loved me. I had a lot of people who cared about me now and I couldn't lose that.

My secrets weighed on me a lot though. I thought a lot about telling, but it all came back to how they would look at me. My sisters always talked about what they would do to a man that molested or hurt their children. It was always some graphic stuff. I was afraid for my life. What would happen to me if I decided to tell the truth? No one would love me anymore and I would be in jail, mutilated by my siblings, if not dead.

I started having dreams about them trying to hunt me down and kill me. I didn't have comfort at home. I couldn't understand why I couldn't just stop if I hated being this way so much. I didn't have a soul in the world to talk to and I just knew for sure that even though I prayed every night, God wasn't listening. At church, I had learned that God doesn't hear the prayers of the wicked. I was beyond wicked.

I turned to the only thing that could ever ease the pain I felt, music. At the time, there was a song called "Nobody Knows" on this album called The Tony Rich Project. I loved that song, mainly because of two simple phrases. They both said the same thing except one word was changed, "and I'm dying/crying inside and nobody knows it but me."

That song spoke to my heart more than anything else at the time. Of course, he was talking about a woman he'd lost. For me though, I'd lost my innocence and it was something I couldn't get back. I felt like I was both dying and crying inside, and true to the words of that song, nobody knew it but me.

One day during Social Studies, I'd drawn a self-portrait. It was a very sad version of me. I drew tears cascading down my face and at the bottom of the page I wrote that quote. I didn't sign my name on the artwork or anything else. It simply said, "And I'm dying inside and nobody knows it but me."

When I got home I went straight to my room. I was going to take that picture and put it in a folder where I stored all my artwork that I wanted to keep. When I looked in my book bag it was nowhere to be found. I panicked because all my drawings and poems were my treasures. Those were the only things that I kept to myself. I couldn't find it anywhere so I hoped that I had left it inside the desk in class.

My Social Studies class was also my homeroom. First thing in the morning I went straight to my desk and looked inside it, but it wasn't there. I sat there wanting to cry, but I didn't. Even Laila knew that something was wrong, but when she asked I just told her it was nothing.

Later on that day, I got called to the eighth-grade counseling office. I thought that was odd because I wasn't in the eighth grade. When I got there, I met a pretty, young counselor named Mrs. Dixon. She seemed very nice and I liked her because she was young and you could tell she was hip to a lot of things that teenagers were into these days. She understood easily how we felt.

She explained to me that I was there because the seventh-grade counselor, who was a man, thought it would be easier for me to speak with her. I agreed and she told me that one of my teachers had found a drawing that seemed disturbing so they brought it to the counseling office. When she placed the paper on the table I saw that it was my self-portrait, I hadn't lost it.

She asked if I wanted to discuss it and if I really felt what the paper said. We proceeded to talk about the same things that I had told Mrs. Steele. I gave her the same story, verbatim. She asked if there was something that was going on now that I would like to speak with her about. She told me that what we discussed would stay between the two of us.

I only told her how it felt to live with my mom and how she held me responsible for the house not being clean and things of that nature. We talked about how she didn't really show me love and how I wished I had parents who did. I even told her about how I used to wish that I was adopted and that my real parents would come and get me some day.

She told me that she had a group of girls who were going through similar things and asked if I wanted to be a part of that group. I said yes, and once a week I got to meet with her and these girls and we talked a lot about things that had happened to us and things that were going on in our households at the present time.

We were all going through a lot. Most of it was on the same level of what I had discussed about my mom so it was a good outlet. I enjoyed being there. It helped me some, but there were still things that I felt like I couldn't share because they would shock everyone and then I would be the oddball. I also didn't want to risk it being spread around school, even though we'd signed a privacy policy there was still no guarantee.

CHAPTER 34

THE BROADENING

After my talk with Mrs. Steele about my past, she seemed determined to set me on a course to experience new things and to help me by providing me with a mentor. The main thing that she kept trying to get me to experience was eating at a full-service restaurant. I was not open to that idea in the least.

Every time I spent the weekend with her we'd always go out to eat at least once. It was always something I did with just her. I still wasn't all that comfortable with Bill and she knew that. Even though I would joke with him whenever he was around I was always far more comfortable when he wasn't. I knew from experience that he was a nice man, but I always thought he had a mean side that I just didn't know about, just like my father. So, I never cared to spend too much time in his presence because I felt like one day I would see that side and everything would be ruined.

I think that Mrs. Steele purposely chose weekends when her daughter and husband were busy to bring me over. We'd always have a short discussion about where we were going to eat and my choice was always McDonald's. She'd express to me that she was tired of eating there so my compromise became other fast food restaurants. Whenever she'd try to wheedle a full-service restaurant in there, I'd shut her down.

One day she really got aggravated with all the fast food and she stopped the car and asked me earnestly what my issue was with them. So, I told her what I believed. Only rich white people wearing fancy clothes went to full service restaurants and I didn't belong there. When she commented that she went there all the time I told her that even though she wasn't white she still had a lot of money and she dressed nice all the time.

She told me that people dress casually to go to these restaurants all the time and it was not only white people who ate there. She'd see black people too. No matter what she said, I just was not convinced. So, she said, "Fine!" She put the car in drive and proceeded to drive to a full-service restaurant while telling me that we were going to eat there that day just so she could show me that I was wrong.

I was terrified. All types of scenarios were going through my mind. I thought that the people were going to kick me out and say that I didn't belong there. They would stare at my hand-me-downs in disapproval. I was sure of it. I worked myself into a panicked state and as she continued to drive I started crying, she was going to embarrass me and she didn't even understand. When she looked over at me and saw my tears again she pulled the car over.

She tried to convince me that I had nothing to fear,

but the apprehension at the prospect of it all would not go away. She just couldn't believe that I was that afraid of the unknown even after she'd explained that it wasn't what I thought it was. She was amazed that I didn't trust her judgment on this.

Finally, she asked what she could do to make it more comfortable for me to go to this restaurant. She refused to let me continue in this same vein. She asked if I'd be more comfortable taking a family member with me. That had never occurred to me, but when she mentioned it, my outlook on the experience got brighter.

I decided that I'd take my little brother Matthew with me. He was in Mrs. Steele's class this year so I thought I'd take someone she already knew. She also invited her husband to come, but for once I was more comfortable with that because I somewhat felt as if he'd be our protection in case things went wrong. But I also didn't agree to it until she promised that she and Bill would also dress in jeans instead of her ever-sophisticated slacks. She agreed and made plans to pick my brother up the next day. We ate McDonald's again that night.

My first experience with a full-service restaurant was eye opening. We did not get kicked out, but we did get some curious glances. I suspect it was more because of the racial diversity at our table than anything else. Although everyone else was white and their jeans were of better quality than my brother's and mine, Mrs. Steele was right. Normal everyday people ate at full service restaurants.

While my brother and I kept them laughing with our stories and jokes, my eyes were being opened. Mrs. Steele had to fight me tooth and nail just to get me to try something new. And while she was right, I would still fight her at every turn when she'd attempt to get me to try new things. She'd always end up right, but my fight was a testament to how sheltered and deeply rooted in naivety my upbringing was. Most times, my mother did not encourage change and she stayed with what she knew and what worked for her. I was my mother's daughter.

That same year of seventh grade Mrs. Steele decided that I needed a mentor. One that was also African American, so that I could see that everything wasn't as black and white as I thought it was. Her name was Mrs. Thompson. She introduced her to me after school one day and I was given her phone number. I had mixed feelings about this because I thought that Mrs. Steele was trying to pawn me off on someone else, like she had gotten tired of spending time with me.

It wasn't that at all. Mrs. Thompson was there to spend time with me and talk to me about things that I didn't feel comfortable telling others. She promised that what we talked about would stay between us. She also was a college educated married mother of two boys. One of whom, we discovered, I had been in class with in elementary school. He gave her the scoop on me when she told him about me, but she wasn't impressed by my bad behavior.

She came to spend time with me once, but her schedule

was so busy with work and family that all our other communications were always by phone. I liked Mrs. Thompson. She'd always tell me that I was the daughter she never had. We'd talk about a wide range of things, but as usual, I never felt that she could take my secrets and still look at me the same. So, I hid from her what I hid from everyone.

My relationship with Mrs. Steele stayed the same. She continued to open me up to new things and I continued to soak up all the love she gave to me. Like everyone else good in my life, I stored up all the smiles and good times and put them in my dream box where I'd take them out later. Always, when I was alone I would have my memories and dreams. I lived in a different world inside my head than the reality of my home life.

CHAPTER 35

EMPLOYMENT

Before the summer came I learned about a program called JTPA, the Junior Training Participation Association. I learned about this program because kids from my neighborhood had gone to work the summer before. I think it only required that you at least be fourteen and you had to come from a low-income family home.

I had missed the opportunity the year before. I had been highly upset about it because you got paid an hourly wage. Mom always said that if you didn't like the clothes she bought you then you needed to get a job and buy your own. That was the driving force in me wanting to get a job. This year I was determined to do so because I hated, I mean absolutely loathed, the clothing she bought me for school every year.

At the end of my seventh-grade year I made sure that I was in the program. It gave jobs to teenagers in poor neighborhoods. It was meant to give us some on-the-job training, an experience that would hopefully open our eyes to the possibilities, as well as a desire to work and have a good work ethic.

The amazing part for me is that they picked you up and dropped you off at your job site every day. I needed that a great deal because at this point both Daniel and Derrick had jobs at a fast food restaurant, but had a very hard time getting rides to work. Sometimes they'd end up either walking to work or not going at all. I would've been afraid to walk that far to a job all by myself.

I was so excited to be in this program and ecstatic that I would get paid minimum wage. Back then it was $4.75 an hour. To me that was a lot of money. I was getting paid almost the same as my mom. My thought was that I'd show her. I'd let her see all the nice things I could get all on my own, without her help.

The first few days of the program we were put into classes to learn the dos and don'ts about working, work ethic, and how to spend money responsibly. To my surprise, Tracy walked in the door looking as fine as ever. I was so excited to see him that I jumped up immediately and hugged him despite the attention I was bringing to us.

He was just as excited to see me also and we were inseparable for the next few days. Once during a break in the hallways, we were standing together talking next to a group of other trainees. One of them asked if we were a couple. I said yes and Tracy said no. Everyone in the group looked wide eyed. Some covered their mouths, while others snickered. I walked off embarrassed.

Later, just before we got on the buses, Tracy came over to talk to me. He explained that he thought since we never talked during the school year, that we weren't together anymore. I told him that wasn't true and, since we got that clarified, I asked if we were back together. He told me no, that he had gotten a new girlfriend in school and that he was still with her.

I got angry and told him that he could've called, but he countered that he had tried a few times but we didn't have a phone. This was true, off and on we did have a phone, but it was never for a long period. We always got a new number at least twice a year, if not three times.

Of course, I still thought all of this was not fair and that ,because I came first, he should break up with the other girl. He said that it wouldn't be fair to her and he was right. He told me that nothing was stopping us from being friends though. I did not want to have any parts of being his friend. I felt wronged in some way, but I couldn't bring myself to tell him so again.

After that we were assigned to work at the courthouse. We were given different offices to work in to my relief, but every day for lunch in the cafeteria he would seek me out and sit next to me. I hated it, but he seemed to love talking to me.

Everyone who saw us together, including some of the staff would ask if we were boyfriend and girlfriend and I'd have to say no. The following remark would always be that it didn't appear that way to them. I'd always think to myself that they should try telling Tracy that.

Aside from Tracy, it was fun. I absolutely enjoyed getting up every day and going to work. I worked in the financial office in the department that predicted how much money they would need for the fiscal year. My supervisor was surprised that I was so interested in the mathematics of it all, but math was my forte. She explained a lot to me and I loved working under her.

I felt very important working there. We lived in a very big county and the court house was huge. It had about two or three stories and a basement that housed criminals going to court. There were a lot of us teenagers from the program who worked there, but the place was so big that there was only one other girl who was placed in the same office as I was. She had a different boss though.

She envied my position because they trusted me to do things that she wished she could do. For the first few weeks I was responsible for shredding boxes upon boxes of county checks. They had the right county on them, but the wrong account numbers so they had to be shredded. I'd end up with at least twenty bags of shredded checks a day and I only did that for half of the day.

I loved it though. I had a key to the room that held all the boxes and was told to never leave that door unlocked if I had to walk away for even a moment. It took me about three weeks to shred them all.

The other half of the day I did desk work. It didn't matter what I did, it was all fun to me. It always seemed to surprise the women in this office that I was so smart. Each time I finished something and they checked over it they were amazed that I followed directions to a T.

Once, I overheard them talking about the other girl and her boss saying that she tried to take shortcuts with everything and never followed her exact instructions. She'd always come by and joke with my boss that she was going to trade us out. It made me feel bad for the other girl.

The only other surprise in all of this is that they all thought that I was so cute. That's not what I'd been told for what seemed like my whole life. My boss and a couple of the other women would lightly pinch my cheek sometimes and marvel at how smooth and baby-like my skin was. Sometimes they'd ask me if I used something special on my skin. Their fascination with my skin and cheeks was very odd to me. One of them even said that it was because I was black. It was strange to have someone covet something of mine.

The attention made me feel very good about myself. I was glad that they liked me, happy that I pleased them in so many ways. At the end of the summer they were sad to see me go and even threw a little office party with parting gifts. I found that I didn't want to leave either. I even asked if I could be hired on permanently, but I was not allowed to work through the school year at my age. I had just turned fifteen.

I had saved most of my money over the summer and armed with close to $600, I went shopping. First, I went to the mall thinking that I would get so many nice things. I didn't end up buying anything there because I felt they were too expensive and I didn't want to part with so much for something I only kind of liked.

The only thing that I did splurge on was my shoes. I bought my first pair of Nike's from this enormous shoe store called Just for Feet. I spent most of the rest of it on clothes from a cheaper department store called Burlington's and bought all my underwear and school supplies from Wal-Mart.

Amazingly, I still had a little over one hundred dollars left. I was trying to figure out what I wanted to do with the money. Of course, Mom had the perfect plan, give it to her because she'd show me what to do with it. She felt like I'd wasted my money on men's clothing and name brand crap. But I felt like I did well to have ten outfits, school supplies, and a pair of Nike's.

I didn't give it to her out of spite. I told her that she'd told me to get a job and get my own and that's exactly what I did. I told her she was never going to see a dime of my money. She shook her head and said shame on me, but I didn't feel ashamed at all. I felt angry at her for all the times that she'd taken my money. I was older now and she couldn't just take what I'd worked hard for.

During all this, new neighbors moved in across the hall from us just before school started. They were a husband, wife, two boys, and two girls. The oldest boy and girl were seventeen and nineteen. The other girl was the same age as Karen and the youngest boy was three.

Karen and the younger girl became fast friends. We learned that the family was African. I thought it odd that the little girl wore oversized, adult clothes that didn't fit her and when I asked Karen about it she said that they'd lost her trunk during their move to America.

I felt for the little girl so, the next time I saw her mother I gave her the last hundred-dollar bill and explained that it was for her to get her daughter some clothes. She looked at me oddly, smiled, and then walked inside. That made me feel like she didn't understand what I had said, but on the first day of school I saw the little girl walking home with my sister with a new outfit on. That set my mind at ease.

For the next week, she came home with something nice on so I knew then that the mother had done as I'd hoped. That Friday, as I was going inside, the father hurried behind me and got my attention. His accent was very deep, but he asked if I was the one that had given the money for his daughter. When I said yes, he motioned for me to come inside their apartment.

I was nervous at this request so I followed him just to the door and stood in the doorway. He spoke something rapidly to the older girl. It was so fast that I couldn't even catch whether he was speaking English or not.

After he finished speaking she just smiled, shook her head yes, and motioned for me to come to her. I walked to her confused at what they wanted. She guided me to sit between her legs. I sat bewildered as she took the pony tail holder out of my hair. She pulled a comb out of the box next to the sofa and began to braid my hair.

When I looked up at her father again he gave a slight bow, smiled and said, "Thank you." He then walked right back out of the apartment. I sat nervously, but excited at the same time. This was their way of giving thanks to me. I was humbled at the gesture as we sat quietly, no words between us, while she braided my hair. I had a hard time keeping tears from my eyes.

This meant so much more to me than them giving the money back. I was far happier with this than the money. I had been trying to get Rachel to braid my hair, but Rachel made a lot of money braiding hair. She had learned how to put weave in with the braids and since then she never wanted to do my hair unless I wanted weave, saying that I was too old to be getting just my hair braided.

I hated weave, I never liked anything that was like a false representation of myself. That included fake nails, nail polish, and make-up. I felt like if someone was going to love me, they should love me for me. Not for the long fake hair, the nails, and the make-up that covered the real me. Because of this, she never wanted to braid my hair. I think too, that it had a lot to do with the fact that I couldn't or wouldn't pay her what she wanted.

But here I sat, after an entire summer of begging Rachel to braid only my hair, getting exactly what I had wanted. After a while the older boy came in. Even though he was African he was a typical boy, teasing his sister who never said a word, and asking me questions. When I finally got up the nerve to speak to her I asked if she spoke English. He answered that she did, but she never liked to in front of strangers because of her accent.

So, I sat talking with her brother while she braided. I could tell that she was listening and understood because when we would laugh I could hear a faint giggle come from behind me. When she was done she just handed me my pony tail holder and patted me on the back. I got up and thanked her and she just nodded and smiled.

I slept over at Laila's that next weekend, but on Sunday when I came back she motioned for me to come over again. I did and she braided my hair a second time. This time I tried to coax her into talking to me and she did. She had a very deep accent but when she spoke slowly I understood her easily.

That day when I left she told me that she was going to braid my hair every weekend. When I said she didn't have to, she said she did because I had been very kind. She instructed me to wash my hair before I came over and to buy some hair grease called Sulfur 8. She also told me that I should no longer perm my hair because it wasn't good for it. From here on out she would take care of my hair.

I listened to her and true to her word she took care of my hair. It grew faster and longer than I'd ever seen it before. I was very grateful for what they were doing for me. The hair growth always tempted me to perm it and see how long it really was, but as long as she braided it, I would never perm my hair out of respect for her.

CHAPTER 36

THE BREAKING

Eighth grade came and I had my new, name brand clothes and shoes that I had bought with my own money. Clothes from the men's section, clothes that I felt comfortable in. I was finally physically comfortable at school. I also felt like I fit in a little more now because my clothes sported names and emblems like most of the other kids. It didn't matter that I was the only girl dressed like a boy, I was comfortable.

The only thing that did start to bother me that year was that the boys were all about having girlfriends and vice versa, but they were never interested in me that way. As before, they'd always express that the sexual interest was there, but no eighth-grade boy wanted to be seen in public with a fat girl who dressed like a boy. Laila would always say that if I dressed like a girl, the boys would ask me out, but I knew better. No boy would ever be caught dead with a fat, ugly girl. Laila was just too nice and she always thought the best of me, she never saw size.

So, my depression continued, everything continued as it had been. Daniel was still relentless in his pursuit of sexual intercourse and I was still adamant in saying no. Now, I was fifteen years old and Daniel was eighteen, still with no girlfriend in sight for him.

As I grew older, my sexual appetite never changed, but with puberty other things happened. I had my first cycle at the age of fourteen. It came in February and went away again as if it never happened. I started to wonder if I'd had a real period. I was happy that it didn't come back though. It was a very painful experience with the cramps and bloating. Mom seemed to think it funny that I was going through it. I didn't see the humor in it at all.

It didn't come again until the next February when I was fifteen. As before, it went away and never came back. I thought it odd, but Mom didn't seem worried about it so I didn't think much of it either. I thought that I was blessed to only have that thing once a year.

So, having a cycle really didn't put a hold on any sexual activities seeing that it made a rare appearance. I continued to argue with Daniel about him wanting to enter me. But there's one day that ended that argument forever. It was in September, we were about a month into the school year when it happened.

I got off the bus from school and I had been aroused that entire day. I had days like that and I couldn't wait to get home. Mom was at work and I was hoping that as soon as we got to the apartment the other boys would drop their book bags and run right back outside. Karen wouldn't get off from school for another hour so, if I could get Daniel's attention without the other two noticing, no one would be there except us.

When I got off the bus I gave Daniel the look and he nodded. We had gotten so used to doing this now that words need not be spoken. When we got to the apartment, as I had hoped, Derrick and Matthew dropped their bags and went back outside to play while Daniel hung back.

We went into my room so that it was close enough to the front door to hear someone come in, but far enough away to right ourselves before someone came around the corner into the hallway. There were no words, I pulled down my pants and underwear and lay on the floor while he unzipped his pants and pulled out his penis.

He lay on top of me, but before we started hunching he asked the same question he'd asked for the last two years, "Let me stick it in?" With my usual frustration and disgust, I told him no, and he sighed and began to hunch with his penis tucked firmly against the lips of my vaginal area. My focus was totally on the feeling and reaching release, I wasn't paying attention to much else.

He stopped a little while into it and said that it didn't feel right and that he wanted to adjust a little. When we did this I always had my legs closed and his were open on either side of mine. This day he asked if I could open my legs a little so he could slide his penis down right in between my lips.

I did what he asked and there was a definite difference that I knew would change the way we did this from here on out. Truthfully, this was a very good feeling to me. So much so that I would reach my fulfillment faster than I usually did and hopefully before he would. Even though now my body was producing large amounts of its own moisture, I still didn't like when he climaxed and it came out all over my private area.

My mind was on those two things when suddenly his body slid down mine and he pushed upward instead of down as he had been doing. That changed the position of his penis from sliding adjacent to my lips to heading straight for them and easily moving past them because of the wetness coming from me.

Immediately I felt a splitting pain as his whole body went solid and he started growling. Horrified at the pain and the change in his demeanor I shut my eyes and bit into my lip. I couldn't register anything fast enough. Before I knew it, he was sliding back out, but just as quick he came back. I felt like he was trying to ram himself into me as far as he could. It felt like he was ripping me apart.

I couldn't hold the pain in any longer, I started to whimper and cry out with it. He just kept going as if he didn't care that he was hurting me. I couldn't form coherent words, the only thing I could remember saying was, "Ouch!" every time he pressed forward. It didn't subside, the pain, every thrust seemed like he was ripping me anew, as if it had never occurred from the thrust before it.

I wanted it to stop, but I just couldn't gain enough strength, I couldn't gather enough of myself together before the next intrusion. Every single one was just as excruciating as the one before it and the helplessness was overwhelming and infuriating. He just kept growling and thrusting.

On his way out I tried repeatedly to push him off me, but to my horror, my efforts did not budge him, not even an inch. I was a very strong, sturdy girl. I always had been and it was terrifying to know that I had no power over this situation at all. I was being utterly dominated and I could do nothing about it. Every effort to push him away was robbed from me by the pain of each violent stroke.

All of it was too much to take in and as the last vestiges of what was left of my innocence, of my essence, was taken away, tears began to fall. There is no way to describe the calamity, the devastation, the hopelessness, the depth, even the death of myself in that moment. There are no words that could ever encompass everything that was taken from me in those few moments of time. To put it simply, the light inside of me was put out that day.

I experienced every sickening emotion imaginable in the span of about three minutes. And then suddenly he stopped, got up, and ran from my room towards the back of the apartment and I could hear him slamming the door to the boy's room. I sat devastated for a moment until I heard jangling as keys were being taken from the lock at the front door. The door had been unlocked and opened, someone was in the apartment besides us.

I ran to shut and lock my door, as I was putting my

clothes to rights the door handle jingled and I heard my mother say, "What you doing in there with the door locked, guh!?" I replied that I was putting on my clothes, but that seemed to alarm her and she started banging on the door and yelling for me to open it.

When I did, she came inside and said, "I wanna know what you doing in here with the door locked, I said!" I repeated that I was just putting on my clothes. She sniffed the air, "What's that smell!?" I told her that I didn't know. She looked at me suspiciously for a moment then left and closed herself up in her room.

Immediately, I went to the bathroom to clean myself up. Even though my vagina was still throbbing with pain I scrubbed the entire area. I wanted to get it off. I wished to God that I could just wash it away, the entire experience, but it was permanently imprinted. I tried not to think about it as I cleaned myself but it bombarded my thoughts and brought fresh tears. I was even helpless against the recounting of it. My mind would relive it whether I wanted it to or not and I hated that!

I sprayed the air freshener in the bathroom and took it to my room as well and sprayed it. I couldn't smell anything but I didn't want Mom to come asking questions again. Afterwards, I lay in my bed with the door locked. Karen didn't come in until it was almost bedtime. I had cried the entire time. And when I knew she had fallen asleep I cried all over again.

That day I had been violated and during that

violation something on the inside of me had broken. Daniel had taken away the last vestiges of my innocence. The very thing that I had held on to and saved for the right relationship was gone. The one thing that I thought that I had control over was not only just taken, but ripped from me. There was nothing left. I had nothing left to give. There was no longer anything normal or good left in me. I felt empty, powerless, and helpless.

* E v e r y   P i e c e   o f   M e

From birth things have been taken

Naked, I came, but mistaken

Mistook for property

A play thing in the making

Not a child, but enslaved a nonperson

To labor in the wages of sin

Producing death from within

A soul tortured in this skin

Every piece of me, every beat of my heart

Every innocent part

Coerced, convinced, and whipped

To rot from the start

Forced and taught to believe

So young and naive

The light in these eyes

They dim with the passing of time

Pieces of me taken

Stolen and traded

Replaced with something disturbing

A problem child in the making

I never meant to be me

Creepy, sinister, menacing me

All the good got replaced
I can't look at my own face
Afraid of what I will see
The loss of it all
Every piece of me

Things to Take
Away

Every child is different, but for the most part, children aren't born to inherently misbehave. In most cases, it is something they have learned or a behavior that has developed from some sort of trauma. Typically, people mark children as bad eggs and write them off. Instead, why don't we delve deeper and figure out what the root of the issue is.

We all, as adults, need to pay better attention. Both to our children and those around us. Gone are the days of it taking a village to raise a child. If it were not for the adults in my life that were outside of my family unit, I would not be here today to write these books. Some of that village living needs to be brought back.

If you know a child that appears to be having some life issues, take the time out to talk to them. Show them that you care about them and what's happening to them. If they don't respond right away, give it time. Eventually, they may trust you enough or feel comfortable enough to share what's on their hearts and minds.

No matter what, above everything else, make sure that this child knows that whatever they tell you will not change your love for them. This is very important. You will never discover what he/she is going through if they feel that they will lose your love or the amount of care/attention they receive from you. Especially if they feel that you are the sole person in their lives that seems to care, unless they fear what's happening to them more than losing you.

Abused children often internalize things, grow shameful, and feel that they are the cause of what's happened to them. If they love the person that is abusing them, they will also struggle with saying something out of fear of losing the person or fear of angering or disappointing the abuser.

Children are being abused in many ways every day. That is a fact, but what we may not realize is that while we are trudging along as adults with so many other pressing things on our minds, it could be happening to our children right under our noses.

So, I thought it would be helpful to share with you some of the signs in hopes to help you or someone you know recognize these signs going forward.

The Signs

- ❖ Anger issues
- ❖ Extremely/abnormally quiet
- ❖ Depression
- ❖ Inappropriate touching while playing with others (ex. Twisting/pinching/squeezing nipples/chest area, touching other children's derrieres/private areas, putting their mouths on or in inappropriate places, hunching/grinding another's private areas)
- ❖ Inappropriately touching themselves
- ❖ Incessant crying and refusing to give a reason
- ❖ Growing sullen/quiet around a particular person
- ❖ Suspicious bruising
- ❖ Body odor
- ❖ Dirty/torn clothing
- ❖ Clothing that doesn't fit
- ❖ Excessively seeking attention from adults
- ❖ Irritation in or around private areas
- ❖ Exposing themselves
- ❖ Fearful/cowering at sudden movements
- ❖ Not wanting to go home
- ❖ Lacking self-esteem/confidence
- ❖ Not wanting to go to/be left with a particular person

❖ Not wanting to go to/be left at a particular person's house

Please take the time out to talk to the children in your life. Whether it's your child, one that you love as your own, or a child that seems to be mentally wrestling for life itself. Pay attention to them, recognize the signs...

*Please note that ANY one sign doesn't mean that a child was or is being sexually abused, but the presence of several warning signs suggests that you should begin to ask questions and consider seeking help.

About the Author

Gabriel currently lives in Covington, Georgia with her wife, Kendell. She drives trucks for a living, which is something she always dreamed of doing. She enjoys writing poetry, reading romance novels and decorating. To find out more about Gabriel, visit

https://www.irisepublishing.com/meet-our-authors/gabriel-singleton

Acknowledgments

I would like to say thank you, first and foremost, to my very first counselor, Dr. Erin Mason. Without your love, voice of reason, and your belief in me I don't know if I would be here today. Thank you for always being my champion and seeing through the mess to find me. Thank you to the best teacher I ever had, Mrs. Sill. You opened doors in my mind that I didn't know existed. Should our paths never cross again, know that I love you and not one word you ever said to me was wasted, you were just dropping advice into my future. Thank you to all of those who believed in me from the start. During my dark days, your words and kindness kept me sane. And thank you to my writing coach, Robyn Robbins, you helped me to have confidence in what God is calling me to do and not doubt myself. To all of you, thank you and be blessed.